Ho...
A Surviv...

I'm sitting on ... ng familial drills i... It shouldn't matt... hat squirts out of a can. Oh, they'll act as though I'm being haughty for insisting on fresh vegetables. I'll just roll with it. They'll tell me I'm too skinny. Dad will worry that my plane might crash, that I could be abducted by terrorists, and about the possibility of another ice age. Everything will have an artificial pine or lemon scent from some toxic product. But this time, my hard-earned maturity will bridge the abyss. Mom will beat me at Scrabble and then rub it in. Horrible, grueling, unnecessary tidbits will be discussed at great length. I will have to learn about at least one amputation. They won't understand why I dress this way.

Oh God. We're landing.

HOME
FOR THE HOLIDAYS

And Other Calamities

Stories By
Chris
Radant

POCKET BOOKS

New York   London   Toronto   Sydney   Tokyo   Singapore

"Home for the Holidays," "Retail Therapy," and "Former Spring Chicken Tells All" were originally published in somewhat different form in the *Boston Phoenix*.

An *Original* Publication of POCKET BOOKS

POCKET BOOKS, a division of Simon & Schuster Inc.
1230 Avenue of the Americas, New York, NY 10020

ISBN: 0-671-56866-3

First Pocket Books printing November 1995

10 9 8 7 6 5 4 3 2

POCKET and colophon are registered trademarks of
Simon & Schuster Inc.

Printed in the U.S.A.

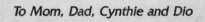

To Mom, Dad, Cynthie and Dio

THANKS

There are so many people without whom I'd have no material, no exposure to readers, no life to write about in the first place. I want to thank Patti Brooks, Jeremy Soldevilla and Caroline Knapp for spotting me early on and convincing me I was on to something; Karen Cullinan and Domingo Pagan, whose basement was my first home in Boston; Tom and Louise Fernandes, Jeannie McGrail, Linda Kugel and Mark Ostow, Michael Melford and Kevin "Dude" Wells, who kept me employed while I was plugging away at this.

Thanks also to Rick and Susan Richter, catalysts and kind supporters; the Hollywood sweetheart, Stuart Kleinman, who got it and persuaded others to do so; Jodie Foster, Peggy Rajske and the movie crew who put up with me in Baltimore and still treated me like a princess; my attorney, Michael Melford; Howard Rubin, who took me under his wing so I wouldn't get creamed in the business world, my agent, David Vigliano, and my editor, Tom Miller, who got the job done and made me look good.

Then there is the army of volunteer copy editors and comma Nazis who removed evidence of my art school education, namely Amy Fonoroff, Susan Sharpe, Kate Merit, Michael Freed and Mark Schruth.

I would also like to thank the Brigham & Women's Hospital, Glaxo Pharmaceuticals and Bristol Meyers, makers of Excedrin.

Most importantly, thanks to Dio, my partner and true love, whose support never flagged through poverty, hysteria, egomania, Monrovia, Pennsylvania, etc; my wonderful "kid" Cynthia Martin, who inspired me to laugh instead of cry in the first place; and especially my loving parents, who've put up with my cantankerousness and sarcastic rantings. Mom & Dad, you gave me everything I'll ever need.

". . . And even if I become middle-aged, which I guess I probably will, that doesn't mean that I'll be one of those strange babes. Does it? I've always been part of the lunatic fringe, but I don't want to be an actual lunatic."
—*Cynthia Heimel*

"What you think of me is none of my business."
—*unknown ancestor*

"Very few people possess true artistic ability. It is therefore both unseemly and unproductive to irritate the situation by making an effort. If you have a burning, restless urge to write or paint, simply eat something sweet and the feeling will pass. Your life story would not make a good book. Don't even try."
—*Fran Lebowitz*

"Just remember, we're all in this alone."
—*Lily Tomlin*

Contents

Contents

Contents

Introduction

From art school to Hollywood in just 25 years.

Yes, you too can rub elbows with Academy Award–winning stars, watch dailies inspired by your very own life and fall asleep at night knowing that you may very well be another Hollywood flash in the pan. Just follow a few dozen not-so-easy steps, take lots of notes and voilà! Fabulousness is yours in just a quarter of a century.

Why sit around your house having a normal life when you could be:

- fretting over how the hell to write a book on high school English alone,

- gripped by terror that your last bit of good fortune was your last bit of good fortune,
- fielding ridiculous questions from *your* pals, who turn out to be star-struck *dunderheads* bent on asking tabloid-style questions,
- wondering if it's too late to work your way up through the ranks at the GAP.

I bet you're thinking, "Hey, I could do that!" Well, I did it, and I say you can too. So get ready to dig ditches, paint apartments, sell a variety of nouns, verbs and adjectives and start that family right now. Get a jump on things by practicing my very own surefire career mantras complete with body postures I'll guide you through:

1) "Anything can happen if you're willing to make something out of nothing." Suggested body language: a grand jeté over a bed of buttercups.

2) "Ignorance really is bliss." Suggested body language: Let the eyelids droop, allow the jaw to go slack and saliva to collect in the corners of the mouth, try not to think.

3) "How in the world am I going to get out of *this* one?" Take enough risks following my plan and you will advance naturally from the obvious head-in-hands position one assumes at the edge of one's bed to a pitiful, high-pitched, sobbing fetal position in full view of a stadium-sized VIP audience.

* * *

Now get ready for 25 roller coaster years of living without medical insurance, job security or any sense whatever of what you'll do when you grow old. Having mastered this, simply pass around whatever type of work has kept you sane and you will have arrived. I know—that's how I ended up with a movie deal with Jodie Foster's Egg Pictures!

For more specific highlights of my own journey to the silver screen, read on, my friends. It really is simple . . . in fact, it was an accident.

Just doin' my job
A groveling appeal for forgiveness.

1995

It has come to my attention that some umbrage has been taken at the inclusion of certain people close to me in the stories I write. I have just spent half a weekend with my head in my hands after learning that an old friend who knows me, knows I love her, and knows how I write, is deeply disturbed to have been misrepresented in one of my little stories. Well, misrepresenting people is so integral to what I do, it's practically my job description. Not that it's my main objective, it's just that by juggling facts, changing responses and being absolutely ruthless about license, I stand a much better chance of making a point, making it interesting and/or funny, and last but not least, making a living. This is not to say that I wish my aforementioned friend had kept her hurt feelings to herself. On the contrary, I was grateful to know I had overstepped my bounds.

I immediately rewrote the story so it in no way resembled the original situation, which I had used as a template for my biting rampage. I quickly removed harsh descriptions which I originally wrote on a dare to myself to push the limits. I replaced them with gentler ones which, it turns out, didn't compromise the overall humor noticeably. As a result, I think the story is improved, and I learned a hard lesson.

My relationships mean everything to me. Who else would have so many complaints and feel so chronically ill-at-ease and neurotic about interpersonal situations but a person who gives a healthy hoot about them in the first place? Still, I may well have become so tuned in to observing life with an eye to the common personal nightmare in every situation that I've lost my judgment for what will hurt others and what won't.

In the beginning of the story "We're Next," I mention that Larry, my neighborhood mailman, smirked one day when we were talking. Was he really smirking? Did I *imagine* a smirk? Beats me! Well, I printed out a copy of that story and stuck it in the mail slot for Larry the mailman. Mind you, the story is about how I and my generation are getting older. The story *isn't* about Larry.

The next day, I saw him on his rounds. He said,

"Hey—I liked that story, but I don't know about that word 'smirk.'" Then I looked at Larry closely and sure enough, he has a sort of crooked smile. Did I accidentally land upon something Larry's highly sensitive about? Does he think that *People* magazine will track him down and feature "the real story of Larry, the smirking Watertown letter carrier?" Will that word cancel out any of the genuine respect and fondness I've shown Larry over the years?

I feel a lot of compassion for that tiny little guy inside everyone's belly who speaks up in a quivering voice and says, "I was just hoping you'd love me and it looks like maybe you don't." We're all desperate little creatures, aching to see a positive reflection of ourselves in this mean world. This I understand. To my mind, that same little voice is the source of what's charming and honest and hilarious about being a measly little human. So in the interest of protecting myself and the people I love best, I feel I must clarify something:

I am not now, nor have I ever been, a journalist.

Accuracy, objectivity and even-handedness are neither among my strong suits nor are they the least bit relevant to my kind of writing. It's important to me to find the most commonly irritating, easiest thing to relate to and to pile those things up in order to give voice to everyone who's ever had a battle with them-

3

selves or had an otherwise really lousy time. You know, the kind of bad day that is so complex that it's nearly impossible to get anyone to listen to it? Well, I aim to speak up for the perennially bugged, the continually misunderstood, well-intentioned clumsy person who will always be on the outside looking in. These are my people. You may or may not want to be counted among them, at least in print. But if you are on the fence, please take a few minutes of your time to:

Complete this simple test to determine if you should take it personally that I've made fun of you or someone whom you believe to be you:

1) Are you in any way, shape or
   form insecure?   __Y   __N

   1a) If so, wouldn't it feel great to
       be able to laugh at yourself?   __Y   __N

2) Is it possible that what I've said
   or implied about you, or a
   character you believe to be you,
   is *true?*   __Y   __N

3) Are you now or have you ever
   been ridiculous?   __Y   __N

4) Have you ever laughed at
   yourself or at anyone else you
   perceived to be, at least
   momentarily, a nincompoop?   __Y   __N

5) Is it possible that events which seem perfectly serious to others stand the best chance of seeming hilarious to you? __Y __N

6) When you give these stories a closer reading, do you notice that the person I most often make fun of is myself? __Y __N

7) Do you think Picasso's models were devastated because they were convinced that Pablo thought they had thick legs and both their eyes on one side of their nose? __Y __N

8) Could you find it in your heart to *get a grip on yourself long enough to determine if you are really any goofier than the next guy?* __Y __N

(And if so, could you ask yourself the big philosophical question: "So what?")

9) When you hear someone say, "Hey—nobody's perfect!" do you think:
   a) ". . . Except me"? __Y __N
   b) ". . . Except Chris Radant"? __Y __N

10) Have you ever heard of making a drawing from a photograph?

Do you think that this indicates
that the drawer thinks there's
something wrong with the
photograph?   __Y   __N

Scoring.
An airtight system of getting to the bottom of this.

Just tally up all your Y and N answers, add the two
numbers to the date of your last menstrual cycle (if
you're a man, just use zero), and divide by the
number of shrinks you've seen in your lifetime. If
your final score falls between 1 and 472, you are a
candidate for the wonder drug Prozac. Otherwise,
please accept my heartfelt apology. I'm sorry if I hurt
you or anyone you believe to be you. I love you and
that little trembling guy in your belly more than you
know.

Who knows why kids pick out certain parental decla-rations and decide those are the most important words ever spoken. My Dad may have also advised me to buy low and sell high, but if he did, I didn't hear that one. I cringe to think of how much worse my life would've been if I had.

The first deadline
Saved by the baby.

1961

Columbus, Ohio, was cooling off after a hot summer, and we were just about to start school again. I remember the stark feeling of disbelief that inhabited my twelve-year-old body. Apparently, I had gotten on my father's nerves and he saw fit to remind me of something—at least he said it as though we'd dis-cussed it before—something, in fact, I had never heard about. He said, "You know you're with us until you're 18 and then you're on your own." And with that, the conversation before and after his statement evaporated, leaving only a whirring sound in my head and a thick feeling in my extremities.

Looking back on it now, I imagine that this was

some sort of standard parenting adage told to my father when he was a young pup growing up in rural Michigan. Back during the Depression, when grandpa either sold his daily catch or fried it for dinner, kids needed to know there was a cutoff point. Times were tough and so were parents. I'd bet good money that Dad simply repeated that statement and didn't even know why. And I'm certain he doesn't remember saying it to me.

But at that moment, I was paralyzed by the vastness of all I didn't know about caring for myself. I was twelve. My legs had just gotten exceedingly long and I didn't look like myself anymore. I noticed my parents didn't pick me up like they used to. And some of my girlfriends were getting bras. I still played on a girl's softball team that went around the neighborhood in the coach's car, honking the horn and waving our gloves, yelling "We won! We won!"

I was stupefied. What on earth would I do for a living? I didn't even know that gas and electric bills existed then, but if I *had* known that much, I'm sure I'd have been stymied about how you get them mailed to you and how you even end up living at your own address in the first place. How our family got to 2358 Park Court I couldn't imagine.

I felt like I was in a dream and might possibly wake up any minute and feel much better. I wondered if Dad and my mother had a secret calendar on which they kept track of the remaining days I'd be underfoot, needing braces, sprouting breasts and apparently bothering them.

Fortunately, my daughter was born just before my 19th birthday. And I've continued to make my deadlines ever since.

The whole time I wrote this tribute to my dad, I kept thinking that it was Mom who did the relentless, the mundane, and the detailed dirty work of raising us kids. Then dad would drop in, make a proclamation and take a bow. Perhaps someday, I'll be clever enough to turn the words patience and love into a compelling story about my mother. But I couldn't do it today. I wouldn't even know where to start.

Chin up, chest out
And other things I learned from my dad.

1995

If I took a snapshot of my father today, he would most likely strike the same pose he held in the photograph I'm looking at as I write this. In this picture, it's around 1931 and he is three years old. He's standing on a rain-soaked sidewalk in Sturgis, Michigan, wearing the short pants little boys wore back then and sporting a very concerned, adult face. It was during the Great Depression. His father's alcoholism had already damaged the family's harmony. His mother would eventually divorce his father in a time when divorce was a scandal. And the turbulence was legible on Dad's baby face. But judging from his stance, William G. Radant was one little boy who could not easily be knocked over. It was almost a military "at ease" position, feet shoulder-width apart, arms casually draped behind the back, with hands cupped together and chin up, chest out.

In some of his Navy pictures, he's standing in exactly the same pose, only he's 17 years old, six feet tall, on leave with his buddies in Hawaii. Now the look of unease in his eyes is a good measure of how far he is from Michigan. I love to hear the story of how Dad got out of the Navy. Every few years, I ask him to tell it again, which makes his eyes twinkle, a wry smile softening his face.

Dad's ability to type (rare for a male in the days before computers) landed him in a secretarial position during the war. Stationed in Pearl Harbor after the bombing, he shuffled papers for Uncle Sam. One of his weekly tasks was to prepare all the documents the admiral needed to sign. For the sake of expedience, he was instructed to line them all up so only the signature line was showing. Then without reading any of them, the admiral would whip his John Hancock on them and send Dad away to distribute them. So when Dad tired of the Navy, with almost a year left to serve, he decided to type up his own discharge papers and included them among the unread documents for signature by the big guy. A buddy of Dad's wanted the same arrangement and paid $15 for it, and they were both out. Daddy-O dusted the United States Navy during wartime and walked with $15 extra. And thus, he became my hero a few years before he even became my father.

When I was born, in 1949, he piloted a small plane

to Sturgis, picked up my Grandpa Radant and flew him to Galesburg, Illinois, to show off his firstborn. Apparently, Grandpa was the only relative to agree to this trip. He, being the aforementioned drinker, knew how to take the edge off such an adventure. During that flight, the legend goes, Dad lost power inside the cockpit and couldn't see his instruments, much less his hand in front of his face. He flew by the seat of his pants, until he had no idea which state he was flying over. There was no way of finding a landing strip, so Dad had to make a crash landing (he corrects me to "emergency landing"), which resulted in the death of several chickens and destruction of a farmer's fence. Dad and Grandpa rounded up the cows they'd set free, agreed to pay the farmer for his chickens and the fence and then continued on to Galesburg once the sun came up again. Talk about flying in the face of calamity. Life would've been a whole lot different if the chickens had lived and Dad hadn't. So when I hear the old saw, "Why did the chicken cross the road?" I think, "My dad was probably flying overhead."

A sense of humor will save the day more often than money can.

My parents had settled in this small Illinois town for the duration of Dad's training as an airplane mechanic. He worked in a drugstore and bought a small plane with three other guys. We had no furniture and lived in a little apartment full of orange crates. But Dad had a plane. Mom supported this on condition that she could gripe about it for the rest of her days. One story from those days tells how Pop risked our young family's meager income by selling douche powder to a guy who came into the drugstore for headache powder, thus proving that my silliness is hereditary.

When I was five, we moved to Columbus, Ohio, where Dad worked for Lake Central Airlines. One of my fondest childhood memories there was going to the Big Bear supermarket, where Flippo the Clown, host of the local cartoon show, was appearing. I watched every day, even after I started first grade. I was a huge Flippo fan. I had even sent one of my drawings in to Flippo's cartoon show and it had been featured on the air.

So Mom and Dad took me to the Big Bear to meet this local celebrity, although in my view there was no such distinction as 'local,' and I figured Flippo probably hung out with Jack Paar, President Eisenhower and Annette Funicello.

My heart got really fast and loud as I approached the venerable clown. I wasn't sure how to break the ice. He *might* not remember my fabulous drawing of a camel next to a palm tree, so I didn't know exactly what to say. But Flippo was a pro and handled the whole thing perfectly. He told me I was pretty. Then he asked me if I was married, which made my knees buckle with laughter. As I tried to collect myself, he gave me a kiss and we said goodbye. All the way home, I was in a star-struck trance, chuckling every time I imagined being married at the age of six. I thought that was just hilarious. Then back at home, I discovered something on my face. White paint! I remember thinking, "Hey, waitaminute! He's not a real clown!" I guess I imagined clowns were just born with white faces, big red noses and ruffled collars. This propensity for the suspension of disbelief has followed me, for better or worse, throughout my life, due in no small part to the fact that I grew up around my parents, both of whom were funny.

Dad always had a frisky, boyish sense of humor. When I was growing up, he repeated the same jokes over and over. If he wanted to convince us to taste something, he'd hold up the substance in question and make like a snake oil pitchman, saying, "Cures colds, moles, sore holes and pimples on the belly." To which we'd all cringe and wail *"Grooooss, Dad! Aauuwgh!!"*

Whenever we drove past a body of water—any water—it could be Lake Superior or a large mud puddle—Dad would say in an excited tone, "Hey, *look,* kids, over there is where Daniel Boone took his last bath!" And we'd smack our foreheads with our palms when we realized we'd fallen for it again.

When he retired from the airlines, Dad bought a luxury trailer home in the Ft. Lauderdale area and promptly installed a shed on the grounds to house his workshop. He took to making crude and beautiful aircraft out of wire, welding solder, gaskets and spark plugs. The bases of these sculptures were chunks of painted scrap wood that were coated with polyure-thane. Later, he moved away from his aerodynamic field of expertise, creating something Mom still refers to as the Awful Eiffel, a squat wire version of the Parisian tourist attraction. He also began to paint along with that guy on TV with the fuzzy hair and soft voice. Mostly majestic landscapes and, of course, aircraft.

I had begun receiving shipments of my dad's 'works' when I was in art school back in the early seventies. He encouraged me to sell them to help pay for my tuition. Over the years, they continued to arrive. Big boxes of wire sculptures and flats full of painted canvas boards. I got another painting in the mail as recently as yesterday. It appears to be some sort of fighter jet with a fierce-looking face painted on the nose, which is intended to scare enemy ground troops. Dad's version of this scary face is a little more towards Barnum and Bailey. The jet is flying straight at me, down low over a range of mountains or perhaps some rye bread croutons, I'm not sure which. This canvas arrived with a written tale about its subject, which is as riotously funny as the painting itself. And Dad knows darn well that I'll laugh.

A couple of months ago, I got a shipment of six paintings from Dad. I treasure these paintings. One is either a sunset, a sunrise, the big bang or an exploding stick of butter. Another depicts a lighthouse at low tide. You can almost smell it. The painting of a field with rolls of hay is truly tranquil, with beautiful colors and a primitive beauty. I called to thank him for the collection. Mom was on the extension line, razzing both of us. When she asked me if Dad had sent his painting of hell with this bunch, I was stuck. Finally, I replied that it was hard to tell, since all of them were somewhat hellish. Daddy found this deliciously funny.

You just do the best you can.

There was a period of extreme unrest that threatened to define us as a family. It was when I was a teenager and couldn't stand myself, much less my parents. And since I was the firstborn, my parents had no way of being prepared for a rebellious daughter, especially one under the influence of the 1960's. So it came to pass that my reputation as a know-it-all, righteous, fussy little bull-headed princess jerk (a reputation I richly deserved) clung to me well beyond my hormone-riddled hippie years. I moved away from my family, just as my father had, at 17. But before I went, I gave them plenty of trouble.

When I graduated from high school at 17, Dad bought me a used car and secretly painted it and fixed it up for me after his long days at work. Then came the day when Mom used some lame excuse to bring me out on the front stoop so I'd see my surprise graduation present. Dad drove towards the house, beaming with excitement. And Mom said warmly, "It's yours, honey." And all I could think of at that moment was that Dad had painted it, of all colors, grey! *Grey,* in the days of psychedelics, Peter Max, VW vans painted with flowers and peace signs. To me, it looked like a utilities car . . . like it would feel as though I had come by to check someone's meter. So, like a knucklehead, I said disdainfully, "Oh—it's *grey* . . ." Mom looked at me with tears welling up and said if I said that in front of my father that she'd never speak to me again, and she rushed into the house.

Honestly, I cannot remember noticing that my car was grey ever again. It was my ticket out, and I had my own chickens to slay, cows to unfence.

Resourcefulness is next to godliness.

My Dad was always making things. Unusual, "experimental" things, some of which were ghastly but more than a few of which were breathtaking. The important thing is that he courted and survived failure fearlessly. During the '50's, he was big on making lamps out of driftwood. He was also a lover of polyurethane and would slather it on just about any natural object to seal in whatever might decay, and to give it a tidy sheen. Mom still tells, with rolled eyes, about coveting something new for our house back in those days, and making the mistake of telling Dad. He would cheerfully volunteer to "make one" for her. Inevitably, "it" would have a tidy sheen and a lightbulb in it. Often "it" resembled some sort of aircraft.

Rather than taking the neighborhood kids and me to the putt-putt golf course for my eighth birthday, he constructed an entire course in our back yard. I remember the split tire that sent the ball in a loop and out the other side, a couple of holes with obstacles (although no windmill) and a bunch of four-foot-tall children wielding Dad's full-size golf clubs. That same year at Halloween, Mom made me a Dutch Girl costume and my brother Jim was a spaceman. Dad made his space helmet out of the box a basketball comes in. Jimmy's chubby little face peered out from the round hole in the box. His innocent five-year-old expression is (in retrospect) hilarious, especially considering that Dad had mounted the floating flusher ball from the tank of a toilet on top of his spaceman headpiece. Aluminum foil was also involved.

I think one of the happiest days of Dad's life was the day he discovered hot glue guns. He glued everything that wouldn't get up and run away when he came lumbering towards it with that look in his eyes. Years later, he was extremely proud of my brother Jim, who had glued two basketballs to his palms for his high school yearbook picture.

Why walk when you can fly?

I remember the day he taught me all about aerodynamics. It was as if he had been waiting patiently for me to reach the age of six or so, so he could draw the profile of a B-52 bomber and make callouts all around the four sides of the drawing marked THRUST—LIFT—DRAG—GRAVITY. We were both sprawled face down on the floor with the paper and drawing instruments. He was so excited to pass this on—the miracle of flight.

*　*　*

In high school, I took a public speaking class, which terrified me. I agonized over addressing the whole class and thought about cutting school that day, dropping the class, and so on. I went to class unprepared and sat there sweating bullets while the teacher got around to calling on me. Just as my mind scrambled for some feeble excuse, I remembered something interesting that I knew cold, and that my classmates had probably never thought of. I picked up the chalk and drew the profile of a B-52 on the blackboard. I wrote the words THRUST, DRAG, LIFT and GRAVITY on all four sides of the plane in capital letters, just as my Dad had done. I aced that speech, and learned a darkness-before-the-dawn lesson:

Stick with what you know, learn as much as you can, and you'll always have plenty to say.

When I was seventeen, Dad took me to a nearby airstrip, where we climbed into a rickety old rented Piper Cub. It looked like it was made out of papier-mâché. He gave me a couple of flying lessons and introduced me to the concept of my mortality during a power-off stall. It was my cut-off point in a series of daredevil stunts Dad had challenged us to when we were young. These were displays of bravery—training so we could "play our edge" in our adult lives. They included such tasks as careening down a 30-foot water slide at the tender age of four, standing up to the bullies in our neighborhood, and learning to drive a tug on the runways at the airport. But I found plummeting silently towards the ground while passing out in the pilot's seat to be too much. I did not hit the ground, but I absolutely hit my limit.

The only thing to fear is fear itself.
(He swiped this one.)

Dad's limits were different. The only times I saw him get scared were the times he *made up* something that frightened him. Like the things he imagined about the Borghese family, a household of Italians who lived down the street from us in Columbus. The Borgheses fascinated my Dad and made him more than a little nervous. He furrowed his brow when he watched "Pappa" Borghese (their grandfather from the old country) take his daily walk to buy a bottle of wine for dinner. Dad thought Pappa Borghese was a wino and commented about it every time he saw the old man rambling up the street and back down with his brown paper bag. Meanwhile, Dad's own father was living with us whenever *he* needed to dry out. And that was enough to make anyone in our family cringe at the sight of a bottle-shaped paper bag.

Davey, one of the Borghese boys, once threatened to spoil my clothes with some paint he got on his hand from my Dad's workbench. I fled, of course, screaming bloody murder like any 12-year-old girl would, and Davey took chase. Full speed, I rounded the corner to the front of our house and tripped on the step to the stoop (Dad had poured a spacious 50's patio that we were all quite proud of) and I fell hard on the cement. Dad, who was reading the paper just on the inside of the front wall, heard both the bone-on-cement thud and the scream of pain that followed. By the time he got to me, I had laid my head on the cement and was crying hard. Dad thought I had hit my head and he looked up and saw Davey Borghese looking culpable, his three fingers dangling off his hand, drenched in blue paint. From there, things turned slow motion and silent. Dad took two steps in Davey's direction, picked him up by the scruff of the neck and punted him across our driveway in the direction of the Borghese house. Davey's arms swung triple-time like the wings of a hummingbird as he fell to earth in our neighbor's lawn.

The next thing I remember, it was an hour later and Mom was attending to my chipped hipbones, which were already showing signs of multicolored bruising. Dad was pacing. He was not so sure that chipped hipbones warranted the boot across the driveway. A head injury, OK. That's what he *thought* had happened to me. And for a head injury, the boot seemed justified—even benevolent. But now he was pretty sure the Borgheses were going to put a contract out on him for kicking Davey without due cause. Dad fretted about this matter on a daily basis.

For this reason, I never told him about dropping a hammer on Joey Borghese's head a year later. I couldn't stand to see him fret like that, so I spared him the details of the treehouse-building mishap that probably prevented Joey (Davey's younger brother) from getting even a high school diploma. I was tossing the tools down from our treehouse and the other kids were snatching them off the ground and scurrying away before I dropped more. The hammer left my hand when the coast was clear, but Joey ran under it and there was nothing I could do. I will never forget the sight of Joey, wobbling to and fro, barely vertical, spurting blood, with his eyes rolling around in his head. I thought for sure Dad was a goner then, and it would all be my fault. I couldn't prevent Mr. Borghese from putting a contract on my father, but at least I could prevent Dad from the horrible suspense of waiting for it to happen. So I kept it to myself, and the Italians never did kill him.

A true hero is hard to find.

Living with Dad made it tough to be impressed with TV heroes I grew up with, like Tarzan, who represented both innocence and naked machismo knowhow. Tarzan had nothing on Dad, who was just as physical, spoke *slightly* more eloquently than Tarzan, and could also jerry-rig just about anything his family wanted, including a putt-putt golf course.

The downside of this came later, when I myself entered the jungle out there in search of a suitable mate. Dad's protective nature, tests of bravery and absolute love proved to be a tough act to follow. And under his tutelage, I had become an independent, ready-for-action little cuss who intimidated men.

You *can* have too much of a good thing.

I moved to Boston in 1981. When my folks came to visit, I repeatedly offered to take them out for seafood, but Dad didn't want fresh seafood, despite its unavailability in Pittsburgh, where they lived then. I could never figure this out, since I knew both my parents grew up on fish caught in the lakes of Michigan. I found out many years later that during the Depression, when my dad was little, Grandpa Radant used to rise early and hitchhike to a lake where "the fishin' was good," fish all day and then hitch a ride back to town (with the same truck driver, as the story goes). Then he'd head over to the fire station where, with a little luck, he'd sell the fish to the firemen and policemen. If he couldn't unload enough fish to buy groceries for dinner, Dad and his parents would have fish for dinner—again. Since then, he had always associated eating fish with the bad old days of abject poverty, the specter of which we lived under throughout my childhood.

This too, turned into an odd blessing. My training in low-budget survival was nothing less than perfect for the life of a writer.

Everybody dies.

That's what he always told us. "It's part of life." And though I dread the day when the shipments of paintings stop and I can't make him laugh on the phone anymore, I no longer believe that dying is the worst thing that can happen to a person.

Dad has always shown a flair for majesty and grandeur, favoring booming Marine choirs over thin folk music harmonies; aerial views over close-ups; full-scale arguments over insightful debate. Here's a guy who goes for his daily walk around the trailer park listening to a cassette of Sousa marches.

So, when given to discussions about dying, Dad has always shown characteristic panache. A Viking's funeral is what my Dad has always fantasized about. He'd like to be laid out on a bed of kindling in a wooden boat and set adrift on the ocean. Then someone on the shore should shoot a flaming arrow that would strike the boat and cause Dad's remains to go up in flames. Frankly, the thought of filing an environmental impact statement on such a funeral is upset enough for me.

I prefer to focus on the fact that creative people tend to live longer lives. And based on Dad's innovations in spelling alone, that indicates he'll be around for many, many, *many* more years. But when he moves on, I know I'll still feel his presence when I fly and when I laugh and when I eat a fish. And thanks to his influence, when life gets tough, at least I know how

to stand: Feet apart, hands draped comfortably behind, chin up and chest out.

My parents sent me a nice card congratulating me
on *Home for the Holidays* (the movie). Dad, who
writes to me once every decade or two, inscribed the
following on the card:

I HAVE A GIRL YOU KNOW
SHE CALLS ME DADDY-O
WHEN SHE LAUGHS OR CRIES, MY HEART JUST SIGHS
SHE HAS HER MOTHER'S GRIN AND HER FATHER'S CHIN
SHE WRITES, YOU KNOW. MOM AND I JUST GLOW
WHEN SHE'D SAY IT'S A PERFECT DAY
WE'D GO AND PRAY
SHE'S OUR DAUGHTER YOU KNOW
SHE CALLS ME DADDY-O

DAD

(Mom signed the card "Mrs. Robert Frost")

One by one, my parents and my kid admitted to me that they had always wondered why I never gave up my life of financial struggle to get a regular gig like everybody else. But since Home for the Holidays, *they're all proud of me for knowing what my true job is.*

The long way is more scenic
Ignoring the well-worn path.

I took a walk in the cemetery this morning with a promise to figure out what the heck has been bugging me lately. Surveying the March landscape, I departed from my quest long enough to assess the many colors of grey before me. "I think I'll go against every aesthetic instinct I have and paint something in all greys," I declared, since there were *so* many to choose from. Then, noticing a family's headstones, I predicted a resurgence of names like Zebediah and Abner.

Now, recalling that my purpose for walking among the dead was to pinpoint a vexing irritation, I circumnavigated a monument surrounded by Japanese maples and came upon a miniature Gothic Cathedral, which despite its lilliputian scale packed the same majestic wallop as Notre Dame or Winchester Cathedral. I stood there, still bugged, and decided that this was not due solely to its architectural style, but also to its surprise location in my favorite cemetery in Cambridge, Massachusetts. Closing my eyes, I recalled, from the many cathedral interiors I've seen in Europe, the wonderful, soaring feeling of looking upward at the flying buttresses that support them. I lingered there before the grey stone building and wondered if this particular cathedral was gargoyle-free because the Puritans, who first populated this area, were so easily spooked. Then I entertained the notion that the Puritans never *ever* suffered with frustration over what to wear. Mind-boggling, isn't it?

It dawned on me, as I focused on what was bugging me, that the very thing stuck in my craw was my *lack* of conventional focus . . . you know, *marketable* focus. My mind ricochets around at spine-chilling speeds, enjoying itself and completely ignoring my needs. So there, in the grey cemetery, in front of a tiny cathedral, I realized that what's been eating me lately is that I'm getting a little scared. I'm 45 now, and honestly, I cannot foresee piecing together an existence this way through menopause and brittle bones.

I guess this is what it means when people say, "the artist must suffer," although I sure don't consider myself an artist. It's true, though, that people like me (whatever you'd like to call us) have a nontraditional way of looking at the world, as though the future will simply take care of itself. I look at the problems facing me in old age, but I cannot feature doing anything differently to soften the blow. I'm just not built for the money machine, which is the only route to security.

Now, before you start to think that I'm doing some sort of veiled bragging about being creative, let me set the record straight. There are pros and cons to having a head like mine. On the bright side, everything seems possible for creative types and life is highly entertaining, even if you never leave the sofa. Then there are the cons. For example, it's damn near impossible to meditate or balance a checkbook. And "other people," which is what the world continually points out they are, have some mighty funny ideas about us. You know, like we all live in cold, cheap places, drink inexpensive red wine, keep late hours and wear berets. They also believe that we are an impoverished people, which is largely true.

Another factor to consider when assessing the pros and cons of the creative life is timing. A mind like mine sees its heyday in youth, where foolishness and lolligaggery have their rightful place. That party is over now. And the freelance life I've led for 20-some years is starting to wear thin. "No, sweetheart, you can't come see Grams today. I was up all night writing and need a big nap." This would be too weird, and it could happen any year now. So I'm at the crossroads, in the cemetery, trying to focus.

A mind is a terrible thing to waste.

You could say that, at forty-five, it's getting to be game point time, and I'm beginning to realize that my strengths in life are to observe, record and make things either funny, emotionally moving or attractive. Have you ever heard of a company that's looking for an employee like me? I need a lot of time alone, a plethora of options, and encouragement to take chances and flirt with failure. Fluorescent lights give me a headache, I like to take afternoon naps, and I find myself to be the best judge of when a day off will enhance the rest of my work. Nothing bugs me quite like a hierarchy. In other words, I'm unfit for normal employment.

Now, as I face my so-called golden years, I realize that despite the numerous applications I've found for my unusual skill set, I cannot look forward to things that others enjoy at the end of a long career—like medical coverage, retirement, and a paid-off mortgage. I'll be seen as the dotty old lady in the neighborhood who must work until I lie down, at long last, on my deathbed. Yes, if there is an afterlife, I will consider it my only paid vacation.

I really should come up with a plan, yet not one bit of success I've had so far has been the result of a plan. I should earn, save, invest, but I only make money in spurts, just in time to ward off disaster yet again. I should pace myself, but it's out of the question, since I must field commercial writing jobs whenever they appear, and work in the meantime, wherever I can.

And when I get inspired, there's no negotiating for comfort. There's only the project (or the exhausting work of *avoiding* the project) interrupted by stints of writing advertising copy, temping, editing theses, paralegaling, writing speeches, naming products and throwing myself into almost any manner of paid labor. I'm always in a dither, either suffering the humiliation of being an imposter secretary or having an absolute blast in my own little world, which is tantamount to flirting with extinction.

Let me describe what's so darned fun about having a creative disposition. From my point of view, it's like I'm facing one of those baseball pitching machines. Every few seconds, I'm launched another bit of stimulus—material I could make into something.

Phooom. Here comes one and "Oh, cool, I think this could be a lovely children's book, with lots of heart and a memorable ending. Maybe I could get my pal Kevin to work on the design, and . . ."

Phooom. "A letter to my mother is what I'm composing now . . . or is it her obituary? Have I prepared my own daughter for *my* death? Wonder if it's too late to swing at that children's book?"

Phooom. "What a soothing pace. These pitches are like my heartbeat. Waitaminute! I *am* listening to my own heart!"

Phooom.

Raw material is hurled my way in a steady, unrelenting, gale-force trajectory. I must judge the input and act quickly before something else takes my attention and I lose forever the sweet moment of thoughtlessly swinging the bat. It's a thrilling state of overload but at the very same time, it presents a string of defeats, of projects that don't get done or don't even get started. It's a protracted heartbreak when once-great ideas scrawled on shreds of paper are found and puzzled over later, when the blessed moment of inspiration has passed and the stimulus is returned to the unnoteworthy domain of everyday.

Even those projects that find their way to completion are then subject to an 80 percent cut, if I'm truly demanding of myself and push to make progress. And as skills are built and accomplishments accrue, one might think that the rewards of these labors would satisfy a creative person. Not necessarily. Even my best efforts may be a source of pleasure for me for a while before the craft I applied to them becomes obsolete, making the whole experience an embarrassment in a span of only three or four years. (The eye gets better by batting at empty air year after year after year.)

This is what you get for the rather godlike endeavor of making something out of nothing and improving with practice. This is the much-envied "creative life." It is the source of both endless pleasure and ongoing financial agony. The "artistic person" stays busy toiling over interpretations of even the most common transactions with the rest of the world. The soul tires of the futility and the struggle to survive the onslaught of missed opportunities and insufficient focus. All the while, you get trotted out at parties and introduced as somebody's friend, the artiste. "Jeez, that sounds so interesting!" they'll say in a giddy tone, their faces contorting. It's either that or, "Oh, so you're a writer, eh? And you also what, wait tables? Drive a cab?" Either way, I feel like slapping them.

How is it that some people end up on this path and others career towards business degrees, paid vacations and houses filled with modern conveniences? I confess I am stumped on this one, though I've retraced my steps a million times, often while sitting in a laundromat.

The first part is easy. Everybody knows creativity is fostered in childhood. Then the numbers of those who'll guard artistic sensibilities during the rebellious teenage years diminish notably as some fall away to sports, security, conformity or oblivion. For me, there was never any appealing option, so I continued to hold my quirky world view in high regard, giving in to it most of my waking hours and, of course, all my dreaming ones; growing up was merely a matter of identifying which was which.

Life was surreal early on, when I was suddenly in charge of myself and my baby girl, Cynthia. By the time I was 20, I was a mommy with three part-time jobs, and a full dose of art school sensibilities. This means that I could be found, for instance, studying such things as how the light fell on a twisted, discarded paper bag near the drugstore down the street from our house. The temptation to run home and fetch some Conté crayons, with which I would gladly touch up the light and darken the wrinkles in that beautiful bag, was overpowering. The idea of subtly enhancing its natural beauty and then replacing it near the drugstore thrilled me. I would actually have grandiose thoughts about raising the aesthetic consciousness of this great nation single-handedly, and unsung. Understandably, onlookers thought I was quite squirrelly, hunkered down there, my baby clinging to me like a little baboon, enthralled by the neighborhood rubbish. Thank heaven, another storm of fascination would pelt me before I could actually get down on all fours to work on the brown paper bag.

This way of seeing the world a dozen irrelevant ways at once delivered me to art school, where I was reunited with "my people" and we were all prepared by the art school staff and by our fellow visionaries to be received by the world with open arms upon graduation. Our special gifts for beauty, meaning, and expression would provide a balancing dose of abstraction for a linear world. Well, you can imagine our dismay.

Some of the most wonderfully talented painters ended up doing portraits at the state fair for $10 a pop. A highly motivated metal sculptor graduated without the financial or emotional resources to obtain his materials and tools. He ended up working in construction, mostly on low-income housing— building boxes instead of sculpting. His soul died long before he drank himself to death. One of my best friends from art school put a gun in her mouth and pulled the trigger, after giving birth to twins and being separated from the world she had flourished in. I was among the more fortunate, both blessed and cursed with only a moderate talent that spread itself thinly over several media. Add to this the fact that I became a mother at the age of 18 and *voilà!* The need to combine art and commerce, whatever way I could, was revealed to me.

Making a living from the right side of the brain.

After three years of art school, raising a young child alone, and the three part-time jobs it took to pay for everything (rent, babysitter, paints, brushes, turpentine, food), I neared the place where ambition ends and breakdown begins. I realized that I would have to find a job for my meager talents in the world of time sheets and cost-efficiency. When I came upon the words "Art Department" it made me think I'd found a place to merge my world with the concept of income.

The ad agency prided itself on creativity. And they actually paid me, supplied me with markers, drawing board and T squares. I was deliriously happy until I realized that men in vests would stand over my drawing board and tell me how to illustrate things. Thus began my lifelong task of duking it out artistically in a money-driven, ugliness-tolerant literal milieu, a place where making something out of something else passes for art.

Having pointed to the disparity in these two different worlds, I will spare you any more details, leaving them to your imagination. Suffice it to say I do not recommend that the uninitiated attempt any of the above. I think the only people who can survive this ordeal are the people for whom there are no other real choices. Born-again philistines who claim to find their artistic voices in midlife are well advised to keep their traps shut around me to avoid my severe grumpiness.

It took me more than 20 years to concede that the guys in vests were right and I was wrong. This is because in the commercial world, it's necessary to present things that people have seen before, so they needn't dwell on the concept and can get right to the business of deciding which shampoo to buy. Believe me, I railed against this till I was bloody. And during that time, I had experiences that made the kooky world of art school look like a bake sale.

For instance: I played a nun in a Mr. Rent-a-car TV commercial which was, please note, *not* my concept; I auditioned to be the voice of a rug in a radio commercial; I've written riveting pieces on antique maps and tiles, and a fascinating treatise on collectible cranberry paraphernalia:

"Early paintings of cranberry bogs show Cape Verdean workers on hands and knees, laboring

*under the supervision of 'Swamp Yankees' with
clean hands[. . .]"*

A regular contributor to the *Boston Phoenix*
newspaper's "Best Buys" column, I wrote a slew of
product pitches, five of which added up to a full page
and paid $150:

*"Between the dry heat and wicked cold climes,
winter can be tough on a New Englander's nose.
Bread & Circus sells Naturade Saline and Aloe
Nasal Spray that reduces swollen sinus tissues
while it keeps the northeast passages clear." [. . .]
"Got a limited budget and a chocolate monkey on
your back? Check out the Borden Candy Products
Outlet at the corner of First and Cambridge
Streets." [. . .]"This self-propelled ball provides
some exercise for pets and fascinates small kids for
long stretches of time. . . ."*

I scripted and produced a videotape for students at
a private detective school; I've named cleaning
sponges, banks, and Band-Aids for $75 an hour. I
wrote for a company that delivered withered roses,
deceased fish and other unwell wishes to anyone the
customer was pissed off at:

*"ENOUGH IS ENOUGH: Creative revenge for
today's world."*

I wrote and produced 50 "history of baseball" radio
commercials for a bank in Cincinnati, researching the

stories with old-timer Waite Hoyt, who had played with (and against) Babe Ruth, and directing PeeWee Reese as the announcer. When I asked if we could be on a first-name basis, he said yes, but when I called him "Pee," he wasn't the least bit amused. I spent most of my energy, during this time, typing with one hand, holding my nose with the other, and trying to keep a straight face.

I flew to Nashville to mix a jingle that boasted:

[. . .]*"the taste that made the south love chicken."*

I wrote copy about hand-carved nativity scenes, including a special savings on the baby Jesus when you purchase the wise men and a few goats. By the seat of my pants, I explained breakthrough medical technology, digital encoding and decoding systems, and Internet services I still don't know how to use. I wrote countless catalogs half asleep, hawking collectible handpainted plates, nose-hair clippers, and vibrating pillows. But more than anything, I wrote parodies of these ads, if any room for parody was left to begin with, and biting little accounts of the humorless people and strange business practices I came across while I was at it. I couldn't afford *conventional* therapy.

It was commercial writing and my subsequent commentary, along with a few half-hearted compulsory art school writing classes, that comprised my training as a writer—not exactly a Sarah Lawrence education.

So how is it that I eventually got one of my essays turned into a major motion picture? What path did I take that wound up crossing those of Jodie Foster, Holly Hunter and several other names that make a midwestern girl's eyes bug out? In retrospect, it's clear that I used my aforementioned strengths—of taking risks, looking for what's tender and hilarious about situations—while I missed what might've been lucrative or secure in life. But at the time, and even to this day, I have no agenda, no clue. Just phooom . . . phooom . . . phoom . . .

I've led an adventurous life, which one *can* do on a shoestring budget. This has given me plenty to write about. And writing plenty is the very definition of practice, now, isn't it? Before long, this business of writing plenty had its grip on me, and I began to do other things, such as make a living, have relationships, and study discarded paper bags, in my spare time. This paragraph looks mighty strange in the Education section of a résumé.

As I got better at chronicling these episodes, I began to make copies of the ones I liked, and distributed them to my friends. I did this for 20 years, turning my therapeutic writing into a strange sort of newsletter. (When I hear an old friend say she has copies of my pieces since the 1970's, I cringe and consider getting a nose job and moving to Brazil. I guess this means I've improved.)

* * *

Then came *Home for the Holidays*

In 1989, I Xeroxed *Home for the Holidays,* a grouchy-but-tender piece I wrote about visiting the family at Thanksgiving, and passed it out to my pals, per usual. One of them, Morelli, was a photographer who sometimes shot for the *Boston Phoenix,* Beantown's answer to the *Village Voice.* It was Morelli's girlfriend, Caroline, editor of the Styles section of the *Phoenix,* who read it, just by chance, while it was lying around Morelli's house. She contacted me and said she'd like to publish the piece in the Thanksgiving issue of the *Phoenix.*

I was resistant, though flattered by the idea. I was afraid of hurting my family's feelings. Years of having my writing changed by guys in vests and doing silly gigs for rent money had taken me to a place very near resignation. I didn't need to alienate my loved ones on top of that! How would my parents be able to understand when I was opportunistic and exaggerated for a laugh, or why I juggled the chronology of events simply because the paragraph read better? The *Boston Phoenix* editor had to talk me into it.

My pals Dave, Monika and Matt advised me against publishing the story, calling it "mean-spirited." I felt they misunderstood it entirely. But this shook my temptation to publish it in the *Phoenix* and see if other people would "get it." After a few sleepless nights and verbally securing my parents' permission to make fun of them, I said yes. The aforementioned *Phoenix* editor was kind enough to bring me in and seat me next to her while she edited it. She handled me tenderly, suggesting only minor word changes here and there, and tidying up my tenses where I had overlooked them. Caroline made my first writer–editor experience downright touching.

Home for the Holidays was the first of my 20-some years' worth of work published with my name on it. When the article first came out, an elderly man, worried that his own children might feel similarly torn between love and alienation, looked me up in the phone book and told me what was on his mind. I also received my first fan letter from a guy in New York City, who described himself, sitting in his shorts at the kitchen table on a sleepless night, reading *Home for the Holidays* and laughing out loud. These were strangers who gave me the feedback I wanted.

I didn't send it to my parents, since their blanket agreement allowing me to make fun of them was never put down in writing and, therefore, would not be binding in a court of law.

It was purely luck that landed that same issue of the *Phoenix* in front of seasoned screenwriter W.D. "Rick" Richter—and divine providence that he had a crazy family of his own, about whom he felt similarly. Rick had a hunch that he and I were not the only ones with a love-grate parental relationship of this kind. I'm guessing that he looked at the high percentage of Americans who turn to psychotherapy at some point in their lives to back up his instincts that *Home for the Holidays* had universal appeal.

My second stroke of good luck came when I discovered Rick and his wife Susan to be lovely, generous, encouraging people. Not only did they volunteer to buy an option on something that could've easily been swiped and altered, but they took an interest in my writing, mailed me screenplays to study, and walked me through dozens of beginner's questions about what to expect. This is the treatment I got in lieu of the horror show Hollywood has come to be known as.

News of my option brought on trillions of well-wishers who rushed to warn me not to get my hopes up that *Home for the Holidays* would actually be *filmed,* much less distributed and seen. This is where my art school point of view finally came through: Since everything is possible and I can make something out of nothing, the likelihood of this movie being made was not even a leap of faith. I always knew it would happen. I worried about how my parents would take it when *Home for the Holidays* became a major motion picture. And I kept the whole deal a secret from them for four years.

While Rick's screenplay made its way through development and around Hollywood, he kept me informed of progress and changes. He FedExed every revision to me and asked for my comments, utilizing many of them, along with anecdotes I offered him over the phone, like the scene in the movie where Henry transfers a filmed home movie to videotape by projecting the film onto the wall and using the video camera on a tripod to capture the image on tape. Bill Radant invented that low-tech transfer technique in real life.

Meanwhile, my writing took a nasty turn. Caught utterly off guard by the rush of having my writing accepted on such a big scale, I vowed to draw my advertising career to a close and focus on getting "my stuff" out. With my daughter now grown up, I could take greater risks by doing what I'd always secretly considered to be "my real job"—the one *only I* could do. The result was a paralysis like none I'd ever experienced. The very idea that I could publish my work in a hip newspaper and even attract Hollywood's attention threw me into a wretched state of writer's block for about a year. Suddenly, when I heard the "bing" tone of my Macintosh being booted up, I was stymied by marketing questions about my target audience and general appeal, rather than enjoying the unself-conscious, conversational flow I'd always experienced in the past. I remained in a stall, with only the occasional piece presenting itself to me to be written. I published several more *Phoenix* articles, but with much more of a struggle.

At one point, I filled out bankruptcy papers and then turned them into confetti in a fit of pride. I qualified for free care at one of Boston's finest hospitals and began taking every type of gig I could, including temporary office work, babysitting, painting apartments, running off to work for the Rolling

Stones in 26 major European cities, and editing other people's work. I even dug a 26-foot trench for $8 an hour. Anything but the easy (and seductive) money I could make in advertising. That made sense while I was a single mom, but not now.

Rick's revisions arrived regularly by Federal Express. He generously walked me through the many steps the script took and educated me in the ways of the movie biz. I continued on, writing, word-whoring and taking odd jobs. I began working in the office of the entertainment lawyer who had negotiated my contract with Rick. Naturally, it griped me, because this lawyer, though distinctly vestless, was a stinker for trivia like spelling and complete, bland sentences written in a bizarre legalese, which is anything but to-the-point.

As soon as I had a regular income again, my old frisky mind returned to me. One day, as I typed a contract for him, the children's song, "Do your ears hang low?" looped in my head.

Do your ears hang low . . . do they wobble to and fro? Can you tie 'em in a knot, can you tie 'em in a bow? Can you throw them o'er your shoulder like a (yadda yadda yadda)—Do your ears hang low?
"Hello, Michael Melford's office."

I'm quite sure I drove Mike up the wall, over-compensating for my non-linear mind by taking whatever he said literally, often to the absurd. It bugged me severely to be a mediocre paralegal when I felt

I was pretty good at "my real job." So Mike and I spent whole afternoons furrowing our brows and sniping at each other. One day, we just agreed to stop our arrangement.

Finally, in August 1994, Jodie Foster's production company, Egg Pictures, exercised the option they had bought from Rick and I accidentally made quite a bit of money with my unruly mind. They announced that principal photography would begin February 15, 1995, in Baltimore. I was invited there for the exterior filming, and to L.A. for interiors. I eventually wrangled myself a job on the set, thinking I'd rather be a hard-working member of the "family" than a useless, self-conscious gawker. Producer Peggy Rajske agreed to let me be a set production assistant, where I would always be in the middle of the action.

Starting in mid-January, I began to plan my trip to Baltimore. I ordered a space heater that plugs into the cigarette lighter of my 10-year-old heatless Subaru. I also bought a mat made of space-age material that regenerates body heat. It was designed and marketed for a pet to lie on, but I planned to sit on mine. I made a drawing of my garments, linking possible outfits together with lines and arrows. I ordered the maps from AAA and sent for information on a women's rooming house. I even bought foul weather gear and pretended to shop for walkie-talkies at Radio Shack, so I'd be somewhat familiar with them on my first day of work.

* * *

I love an adventure.

I was about to become the oldest set p.a. in the history of the cinema, in a city where I knew not a soul, shooting exteriors in February, and I couldn't have been more thrilled. Due to all my preparation and world experience, I just knew I'd make a great production assistant. I could barely wait for the extraordinary experience of watching a movie being made about a family somewhat like mine, starring Holly Hunter, Anne Bancroft, Charles Durning, Robert Downey Jr., Geraldine Chaplin, Claire Danes, Cynthia Stevenson and Steve Guttenberg, and directed by Jodie Foster.

As a little girl in Ohio, I remember selecting fantasy family members and daydreaming endlessly about my life with them. One of my families consisted of Bill Cosby and Dale Evans as parents, with Rootie Kazootie and Lambchop as siblings. I could never have dreamed up my *Home for the Holidays* family, though.

Twenty-some years of writing for no apparent reason finally brought me *Home*.

In retrospect, I can see I've often pulled some sort of nutty when my friends have gotten married. I think I'm just grouchy about that wedding of mine. And for all of these things, particularly the latter, I am truly sorry.

Carla's last wedding

Comparing the fête to the facts on one trip to Florida.

1994

Used to be, I loved going to weddings, where I inevitably got all choked up over the sacred vows and a little breathless at the splendor of it all. For most of my life, I've been a sap about The Big Day. But somewhere along the way, I've changed. *Man,* have I changed!

I've just been to a wedding in Sarasota and a 24-hour side trip to visit my folks in Ft. Lauderdale, all of which has served to reconfirm my impatience with family members and contempt for the general public.

The happiest day of my life.

The wedding, Carla's third, was tasteful enough, conducted under swaying Spanish moss in a gazebo that was all twisted up with sparkly little Christmas tree lights. Due to the low lighting, the bride and groom were barely visible, but all the better, since Carla's bridal costume, containing far more synthetic material than Carla would normally be caught dead in, might've looked somewhat cheesy under much more wattage.

As for Sarasota, I must admit to succumbing to major culture shock. I could not get used to the leisurely pace and the seemingly friendly patter about nothing in particular. In my world, the only people who chat it up with you in this manner are about to hit you up for money. I could only imagine that it was that or some sort of covert hostility and *not* honest-to-goodness honesty and goodness. Naturally, this says more about my own shortcomings than it does about Southerners.

The bride, a Southern belle herself, imported only a few other crusty New Englanders to the bash, so my reference points were few and far between. Fortunately, though, I found some childhood chums of the bride who suited me just fine. Sonya, a six-foot tall veterinarian whose special interest is primates, was quite entertaining as she bubbled on and on about monkeys and intermittently spewed venom about "Min!" (Men.)

Barbara, Sonya's great friend, also from South Carolina, conducts reproductive endocrine research on rats. Both were fun to hang around with, especially since their interests provided an outlet for my hypochondriacal anecdotes. This made for lively conversation. I even made them laugh a little, which always puts me at ease. Still another grade-school chum of Carla's was a charming and extremely well-preserved 46-year-old single flight attendant, with superb taste in clothing. She kept the men in attendance busy, craning their necks and thus sparing the rest of us requests to dance at the reception. I think envy was my only obstacle with Sharon, whose gorgeous presence in the room was felt by all of us at all times.

Every few hours, there were meals sponsored by one family or the other. And the food was downright abysmal. Okay, perhaps this is a function of my snobbery, but truly, the chow available in Sarasota, Florida, especially the food prepared for large groups all at once, is not what I crave when I'm in a strange culture with people I don't know and looking for some comfort. About this, I preferred to gripe loudly (as is my custom when I'm ill at ease) vs. choking the food down. A migraine ensued. I do believe my popularity plummeted. I was later able to rally by telling the story of my movie, which I now keep in my back pocket until I've misbehaved and need to buy back some favorable attention. Shallow, but it works every time.

Carla's five-year-old son from her second marriage was literally crazed by all the aforementioned strangeness, and left to run amok in the hotel where we all stayed. Carla had to choose between mothering him, probably to no avail, or being fully present for this, her wedding day. The groom's family, as well as the rest of us, attempted to engage him in any type of conversation or activity that would distract him from what must've seemed like a nightmare to him. But his eyes glazed over, and no one could penetrate the numbing self-induced fog he surrounded himself with, poor kid. Carla looked high and low for a doctor to advise her about the proper dose of Valium to use to drug him for the duration of the ceremony. (The Valium was supplied by one of the great aunts who's terrified of flying.) Judging from the boy's behavior, the drugging never took place. However, *I* toyed with finding the great aunt and hitting the old girl up myself. I'd have been perfectly happy to sit in the corner of some anteroom with a five-year-old in a suit, ripped out of our minds on Valium and commiserating, "Hey, where do *we* fit into this shindig, anyway? The only person *we* know here is busy pledging her love to some *guy in a tuxedo!* And why is everyone being so *congenial?* Isn't it too perfectly goddamn clear that this is *agony?*" And then we'd toast the bride with some apple juice and have a good cry.

Despite my personal alienation, the wedding and reception went off fairly smoothly and I managed to get a ride back to the hotel early with the children, claiming I was inspired and needed to write. (I find that people love to believe that romantic muse stuff about writers.) The truth was: a) I needed to cancel out all that disingenuous smiling and feigned interest with some alone time and b) I was woozy from my new bifocals. So I went to my room, bathed, took a muscle relaxer, putzed around on my computer, and watched *Saturday Night Live,* happy as a clam, until my hotel roommates (other girlfriends of the bride) returned all sweaty and drunk from the reception at 1:30 A.M.

The next morning's annoyances were limited to food, nausea, and group dynamics, chiefly that we couldn't locate the flight attendant, who had apparently fallen in love and abandoned her hotel room. Also there were a few grumbling, hung-over receptioneers whose backs ached from doing the limbo the night before.

Then, as a pre-emptive strike (so there'll be no question about a holiday visit), I flew to Ft. Lauderdale to visit with my parents for approximately 24 hours.

Enter Hurricane Gordon.

Actually, the pounding wind didn't increase the chaos measurably at the Radant estate. The TV is always played at full volume, causing the entire trailer to throb and rattle, so we couldn't hear the storm much anyway. And of course, my parents conduct a running commentary on whatever's going on at a few decibels above the TV, e.g.:

MOM

(hollering in a tone similar to Ethel Merman's):

"Bill—I called our insurance company to see if we're covered in case that big tree falls on the carport, and the girl at the office is going to call me back, so when the phone rings, I'll get it."

DAD

(from the far end of the trailer, where the radio's playing "Oh, what a beautiful morning"):

"WHAT?"

MOM
(louder):

"I said I called our insurance company about that big tree falling on the carport, and Vickie's going to call me back!"

DAD

(alarmed, as though one of his imaginary emergencies may at last be happening):

"Who the hell is Vickie? What the hell fell?"

All of this, drowning out an important TV news clip about flight delays and the storm. And things went on and on like this, as they always do.

51

Finally, time to go back to the airport.

After running the usual gauntlet of questions fit for a traveling four-year-old: "Do you have your ticket?"; "Is Dio picking you up at the airport in Boston?"; "Do you have enough money?" and "Did you remember everything?" I made it to the terminal with my tongue pinched firmly between my teeth. Dad put my bag on the sidewalk and they both kissed me goodbye in the howling wind and rain.

Then, in order to avoid the huge crowd at the curbside check-in, I headed for the terminal door to the left of the one marked USAir. For me, it is perfectly normal to walk a little farther to avoid a crowd, and I would simply do a U-turn inside and head for my gate. As I walked toward that door, I swore I heard both my parents bellowing my name and whistling loudly. I ignored it at first, hoping they would regain their composure and possibly even realize that, with all my life experience, I could handle things from here on. But their urgent calls became louder and more insistent, so I turned around to prevent them from lumbering after me like I was a blind woman walking into a rush-hour intersection. I'm sure the look on my face was a disdainful one as I made eye contact with Dad. And sure enough, he was pointing toward the terminal door on the far side of that curbside crowd. I assured him with a brusque hand gesture that he should go home.

At that point, I should've savored the relief of being inside the terminal, but I was losing it. Storming through a terminal full of Floridians and tourists, muttering to myself and wishing I were home, I appeared to be quite crazy.

By the time I boarded the plane, I was utterly overextended. I mistook the seat a woman was sitting in for my own, and said (sweetly enough, I thought), "I believe I am assigned the seat you're sitting in . . . 13A." To which her male companion said, "That's the window seat, honey, not the aisle." So I snapped back at him with a smirk, "Oh, you're calling *me* honey? I thought you were speaking to your *wife.*" And the wife piped up, *"I'm* honey!" pointing to her own sternum. And so it was we began our flight through a hurricane, side by side, cheek by jowl, me and honey and her husband. You could cut the tension with a knife.

I have no idea how I got this way. Not so very long ago, I blubbered at weddings and thought people in general would be really interesting to chat with. Alas, I find I am no longer cut out for the random stranger, let alone an entire weekend full of them. It's a darn good thing I can't drink, because I yearned for a cocktail *so* many times in the last 72 hours. I'm quite sure I'd be a menace to society if not for my migraine problem.

As for the institution of marriage, I may *still* be too young. When I ponder my own future vis-à-vis wedded bliss, I wake up at night worrying about turning into Mr. & Mrs. Honey or bellowing at each other about insurance the way I heard Mom and Dad do.

I'll wait and see how it goes with Carla first.

Company comin'
Nothing gets the house cleaned faster.

1956

We had one of those snappy red 50's wall phones in our kitchen. The receiver was heavy and hung on a chrome armature. There was nothing unusual about it ringing regularly or about watching Mom's hand snap it up and cradle it with her shoulder. The cord, always desperately tangled into an exploded softball shape, must've been about 30 feet long, because Mom walked all over the house talking to her girlfriends, whose names were Ernie (Ernestine) Fearing, Marty (Martha) Murphy and Myrt (Myrtle) Gatton. For my younger brother and me, there was a sense of being "off duty" when Mom picked up that red phone. She was likely to be occupied for long stretches of time, engaging in conversations that made her voice dip down to a discreet whisper, then cause her eyebrows to rise up just before a laugh.

But when the phone rang this time, it ignited a flurry of panicked activity. Suddenly, we were instructed to dust mop the floors along the woodwork, pick up our toys and Pledge the end tables. Grandpa, who was living with us after another one of his "illnesses," began shaving and putting on a proper shirt. Mom focused on making tuna salad sandwiches while she supervised the rest of us.

All we could get out of her was that Dad had called from the airport and told Mom to get everybody ready to meet someone he was bringing home for lunch. Mom obviously thought it was a business lunch, the success of which might determine Dad's future at Lake Central Airlines. (Hence the tuna fish sandwiches with the crusts removed.) So we whirl-winded the house and combed our hair and became as nervous as kids can get about a business lunch at the ages of three and five.

When everything was clean and lemon-scented, we began watching for Dad's black Ford to come down the street, so we could preview this V.I.P. guest. But when he finally pulled into the carport, it appeared he was alone.

Dad wore a bomber jacket to work in the winter time. It got cold in those hangars in February. And he was good at dressing for the weather, always zipping and snapping things shut to ready himself. And that's the only thing we noticed when he trudged through the snow, up the front stoop alone: His bomber jacket was unzipped down to his mid-torso. And something resembling a licorice gumdrop, surrounded by fur, was sticking out.

It was Pepper's nose. Dad had found her in a snow bank out by the runway. She was barely more than a handful of dog. But that's all my brother and I needed to take us through our growing up years and keep us company.

Mom and Grandpa were really grouchy about having cleaned up in such a hurry.

*I stared at a globe from about 1956 to 1968, when I
had my kid and became otherwise distracted. Finally,
in 1990, with Cynthia grown up and gone, I hooked
up with the Rolling Stones and got to see the world
close up.*

Hitting the road
(the road hits back)
My summer with the Rolling Stones Tour,
Europe.

1990

I suppose you could say that I overreacted to the onset
of midlife crisis. Running off to Europe to work with
the Rolling Stones is not standard procedure. Most of
my contemporaries began their crises with an expression that's straight out of the book. You know: phallic
car. Mid-life tattoo. A sleazy affair. I just happened to
be in a funny place at a funny time.

See, a friend and I had been griping about work
situations. I bellyached that the many frustrations of
being a freelance writer had been made even worse by
Massachusetts' formerly miraculous economy. He
was steamed about his partner quitting just before the

European leg of the Rolling Stones' tour. Well, one thing led to another and before I knew it, I was boarding a plane to New York in full interview regalia. All quicker than you can say "imposter."

The job title "Travel Advance Person" meant nothing to me at all. Beyond being a person, I was completely unqualified for the job. But I'd gotten a whiff of adventure just at the moment of burnout and this minor detail about aptitude was not about to stop me from sniffing around a bit.

My interview with the tour's organizers was about as silly as the notion of running off with a rock band in the first place. Two men with bloodshot eyes walked into the room. One of them glanced down at a piece of paper with my first name written on it and said, ". . . So . . . (pause) . . . Christine . . . have you ever been in a hotel before? Did you like it?" (Excellent icebreaker.)

These were the questions that would end up changing my life. Just *how much* my life would change remained to be seen. And so did how much I would end up liking hotels.

They explained that my job would be to travel throughout Europe in advance of the Rolling Stones production crew and prepare their 100 rooms in four-star hotels. They warned me that I would encounter uncooperative hotel staffs and occupied rooms before completing each mission. I reflected on the many persuasive techniques I had used raising my daughter and decided I was right for the job. Somehow I managed to convince the tour big-wigs of this.

The next thing I knew, I was on a plane for Holland, where someone named Gunter was going to pick me up and deliver me to the Rotterdam Hilton. (Every other time I'd been to Europe, I camped out on somebody's couch and had taken public transportation.) I remember little more than muttering, "Good Lord!" every few minutes during the flight. And removing the crumpled paper from my pocket to read Gunter's name over and over again.

Even in my bewilderment, I felt hopeful that I would function with a new poise in Europe. I felt certain that being 40 would be much less significant, or at the very least, I could count on a lot of cool architecture to distract me.

I was right about the architecture. Wrong about the poise.

There is an awkwardness that takes over when you land alone, dazed, lagged and somewhat clammy, into a different country. Public doors don't push, pull or slide open the way they do at home. Telephones, toilets, traffic—everything works differently.

You feel like you're wearing huge, flat clown shoes that say "American nincompoop" on them, in neon. There's nothing you can do but stumble about, spaced out, tripping over curbs and not knowing in which direction to look for oncoming traffic. It must be that governments decide things like the official height of curbs and stairsteps, because they all felt unnatural and weird according to my American sensibilities.

With dozens of these things throwing you off at any given moment, it becomes quite difficult to operate in the physical world.

Famished, because it's easier to fast than it is to admit to the waiter that you're (another) American and would like to speak *your* language in *his* country. (It wasn't until much later that I realized how common it is to find English-speaking people in the Netherlands.) And I had to *read* my money. It was all very humiliating.

At one point, I found myself sitting on the steps of something I had finally determined was a library, trying to arbitrarily establish a point at which it was yesterday. I have no clue exactly how many days I wandered aimlessly through public places, hoping I wasn't bothering people who knew what they were doing and how things worked. I just loped through the scenery like an extra in their movie. A mysterious, fogged-in misfit, losing weight by the day.

I had successfully lost my preoccupation with age. I couldn't remember mine. And as the jet lag wore off, my attention shifted to avoiding the shopkeepers and restaurant workers who had dealt with me during those first days there, when I was still doing mime and making artist's renderings on napkins in order to communicate.

I tried to warm up to the idea of starting my new job, but couldn't seem to get a grip on my confidence. I felt it was important to let as much time as possible pass before approaching the Rotterdam Hilton's hotel staff and announcing that I was the "Travel Advance Person" for the Rolling Stones. I was sure they would all fall down laughing. Especially since a number of them had seen me that awful day I arrived, when I tipped *everyone* in the hotel lobby, minced through the revolving door in the same compartment with the bellman, and (ugh!) kissed Gunter. Plus I thought it would be a good idea to stop muttering, "Good Lord!" before I presented them with my calling card.

Time passed and I was still oddly wacked out. I checked one more time for gravel in my eyes and sought some grounding, familiar activities. I started by taking a Valium. I purchased a *Herald Tribune* and eagerly turned to the sports page to see how the Celtics were doing in the playoffs. The headline read, "Celtics Eliminated." And that did it.

A tidal wave of sobs took me by force. Fifteen minutes later, I blew my nose and sat up in bed. Gee, I took it awfully hard about the Celts.

When I finally regained my composure, I sat there still as a snapshot, surveying my situation. I heard the whir of the air-conditioning system, interrupted by moist, urgent sniffs, and saw in the mirror a brand-spankin'-new Travel Advance Person with swollen eyes, sitting on a hotel bed in Holland next to an empty box of tissues inscribed with the words, *"Opheffings Vitrerkoop!"* and a spent sports page.

While my friends back home pictured me slugging

back Rebel Yell with Keith Richards, I sat in the Rotterdam Hilton with Visine stains on my blouse and a Dutch version of *Family Feud* on TV.

And I just sat there, with travel in the big world calling, adventure in the air and show business in my blood.

All together now, "Ooooommmmm"

Let's all go to our favorite beach.

1995

I've been doing this since . . . oh, way back before the harmonic convergence, and I am getting much better, I swear. I've faced my contempt for group activity, and for groups in general, by enrolling in scores of self-reflective courses. Over the years, I've endured the est training, the Forum, Mind/Body Health Management, some women's groups and yoga. I've taken more than one intensive weekend workshop tantamount to a semester crammed into a mind-numbing 56-hour stretch. Now I study the challenging and complex enneagram, an ancient Sufi system of understanding human beings, which I find to be pretty airtight. It has made me more patient with others and it helps me as a writer, too, on those rare occasions when I venture past first person. Far beyond being a legitimate tax deduction, I can say that these workshops and courses have helped me immeasurably to understand myself and my fellow man. That's not to say I *enjoy* my fellow man any more—especially in numbers higher than four or in places smaller than Wyoming. But I understand much more about why they act that way, and why I react to them this way, and why it is they think *I'm* acting and *they're* reacting. Pretty good, eh? And I'm only 45.

Okay, so now I'm in a weekly meditation/visualization class. Only three other women do this class with me and they're every bit as odd as I am, so I'm pretty cozy there. I attend religiously, maintaining a poker face and a secret life as a serious person. I barely ever crack jokes, smack my forehead or complain. But my pride about this subdued outward behavior is still challenged by the occasional appearance of Monkey Girl, who still shows up at serious moments and snatches my attention away from business at hand. Let me explain.

At yesterday's group, we were guided through the following meditation, accompanied by an audiotape of the crashing and retreating Pacific ocean:

Teacher: "Take a few deep breaths. Make sure to draw your breath up through the heart chakra."

You must imagine now: four grown women sitting in an apartment in Cambridge, Massachusetts, separated only by thin panes of glass from the jackhammers, sirens and rooms full of other groups where people chant, weep, and give emotional poison back to their parents. Cross-legged, we sat with placid faces on our side of the window pane and breathed deeply, pretending to be elsewhere.

Teacher: "Now, picture yourself on a beautiful beach."

I rolled my closed eyes, thinking that since I was the only fair-skinned person there, I wouldn't be able to stay as long as the others. Just my luck.

Teacher: "Sit on this beach and see the horizon. Feel the expanse of the earth and ocean."

The only other time I've ever fixed on the horizon line in this manner was in a boat that was riding 10-foot swells in Mexico. I followed instructions and fixed my gaze on the horizon in a vain attempt to avoid vomiting. This sensory memory made me a bit queasy. I hoped the meditation teacher wouldn't guide us to smell anything unlovely like chlorine bleach or wet dogs.

Teacher: "Now just let yourself play out there in the ocean. See what kinds of images come up."

Uh-oh. I see a fish tail sticking straight up out of the water. It's not moving. No coast guard in sight, either. I'm pretty sure the fish is dead. I can't explain why he's vertical. I'm not sure what this means about me.

Teacher: ". . . and when you're ready, notice that a bottle has been washed up onto the beach. It has a message in it. Take it out and see what it says."

Quelle horreur! It says, "I love what you do for me, Toyota!"

I'm not getting good results with this exercise—the others are having a ripping time on the beach and I'm humming a Toyota jingle. What's wrong with me?

Teacher: "Take your time and decide what messages and objects you would like to put back into the bottle before you send it back into the ocean."

This reminded me that I had forgotten to put the recycling out. Nothing more.

Now imagine this room of the four of us. The others were audibly tan. They began to emit breathy sighs and dreamy hums while I blistered, grew clammy, and remained nauseated from the boat ride in Mexico.

Teacher: "Good. Now look off into the distance. Someone is approaching with a tray full of things. As this person comes

> nearer, it becomes obvious that what
> they're bringing is for you. Who is it?
> And what do they have on the tray for
> you? It can be whomever and whatever
> you want."

All I could think of was Prozac and lemon cookies
brought by Denzel Washington.

Teacher: "You can thank that person now."

Thumbs up and hit the road, Denzel. My parking
meter is running out and Monkey Girl has to get back
to Massachusetts.

One of my girlfriends asked me for advice on raising teenagers. I told her:
"You do just like you did when your child turned four. Tell them they have <u>one</u> chance to blow out all the candles.
If they leave a few burning, say, 'One more!'
And 'One more!' And '<u>One</u> more!' until they're all out. Then clap like hell."

Relaxed and refreshed
Sex education and the Single Mom.

1983

It's tough to forget one's own sex education when the time has come to pass the delightful news on to one's own offspring. I myself recall being quite stunned by such information. Stunned and sickened. In fact, I think I must've blacked out there for a while, because I cannot, for the life of me, remember the actual words or the event, or even the exact season of the year that it took place. I only remember sitting on my pink chenille bedspread and staring at the other twin bed for an eternity with my eyebrows pinched together. And life was never really the same again.

Even after I could begin to think about other things,

I'd be caught off guard by yet another disgusting mental image when I noticed, for instance, that the Girl Scout leader, Lois Brooks, and her grubby little weasel of a husband, Charlie, had three kids. Even the minister of our church had done it—I know, because his kids looked just like him. I used to sit in school and space-out in horror with thoughts of my teacher with some naked guy. Ugh! It gives me the willies *to this day* to think of Mrs. Beers, my first grade teacher or—God forbid—Miss Ringenberg! It makes my flesh crawl.

Once I had recovered from the initial blow, I returned to my mother to clarify something that had been bothering me for weeks. "How long does the man have to leave it in there?" I asked her with a voice like a piccolo. At that moment, her face looked like Mona Lisa's and mine looked like one of those malnourished South American children you can adopt for just 70 cents a day. I didn't see *anything* funny about this at all. My mother sniggered at the most baffling times! "That varies," she said, in a voice that indicated she couldn't wait to phone her girlfriends and tell them about this one. I pondered her answer for a short while and concluded that this variation must be the explanation for multiple births. Therefore, mothers of twins and triplets must be the more sex-tolerant women. This thought also made me hanker for a moist towelette.

I thought I would surely spend the rest of my life falling asleep with the word "why?" on my lips.

Then I had a sleep-over with my childhood best friend, Nancy Grady. As soon as we were alone, I held on to both of Nancy's forearms and told her what I had found out about sex. I fully expected her to shriek and run retching towards the bathroom, but instead, she got one of those Mona Lisa faces like Mom had gotten. "What's the deal with that little smile?" I said, smacking my forehead. "Well, it's just that *my* mother told *me* the same thing, only *she* said that afterwards, you feel *relaxed* and *refreshed*," Nancy said with a happy-go-lucky grin. So I shrieked and ran retching into the bathroom.

Behind the locked door, I pouted and posited that everyone but me was in on this wacko sex joke. I imagined that, now that they had all conspired and gotten my goat, I'd emerge from the bathroom to peals of laughter and they'd all slap their legs for years to come and chuckle, "Oh, that sex joke we pulled on Chris was a good one, shooowee . . . !" Finally, Mr. and Mrs. Grady got concerned about my stay in the bathroom and I came out, claimed loudly to be bushed, and went straight to bed.

The next morning at the breakfast table, I studied Mrs. Grady. She seemed relaxed and refreshed, all right. She served us french toast and chirped about what the Grady family had planned for the rest of the weekend. "Oh, I think I know about your little plans,"

I muttered to myself, and ate a second stack of French toast so I could look the sex fiends over a little longer. Meanwhile, Nancy was bloated on her first helping and kept bugging me to hurry up so we could go roller skating.

"Mom, the kids at school are telling wild stories about where babies come from. What's the real story?" My daughter Cynthia looked up at me innocently. *"God,* she looks like me when I was a girl," I thought. I was determined not to make her wig out like I had wigged. After all, I was a product of the '60s and had even fired off a few rounds during the sexual revolution. I represented the bra-burning generation and had cultivated a view that sex was a beautiful thing. A natural thing.

"Well, honey, the truth is pretty wild, too. So let's compare wild stories. What do the kids at school say about sex?" And without flinching, she matter-of-factly told me. "Far out," I replied, because that's how people talked back then, "that's pretty much it!" And when she asked me *why* people did that, I provided for my daughter what was the missing link in my own sex education: "Because it feels good, so they have an urge to do it. And the urge has nothing to do with how it feels when people just *talk* about sex. Like the feeling you may have now, while we're talking about it, is *nothing* like what a girl feels when she has the urge to *do it.* And if you don't feel that urge, then you're not *ready* to have sex." I was pretty sure I had lost her. "Oh. OK," Cynthie said with pursed lips and raised brows. And then she asked if she could watch TV.

For about a year after this initial sex chat, I would, out of the clear blue sky, add tidbits that I thought might also be important, such as, "Hey, you know, a girl only gets *one first time.* So it's important to make some grown-up choices about that first time so it's a wonderful memory forever." "Maaa-aam!" she'd implore, "can't we talk about this someplace *else?* Everybody in the grocery store can hear you!"

"There are three things to keep in mind in order to make your first time a pleasant experience," I'd say, studiously avoiding the words "relaxed" and "refreshed." And with that, I would launch my dissertation on unwanted pregnancy, disease, and a broken heart. "I'll tell you all I know about how to avoid these Three Things, and then when it's time, it'll be *your* job and *your* business to manage it so it's a pleasant experience. And by doing that, you'll influence what kind of role sex will play in your whole life. It's an important responsibility." I figured at the very least we could remove the temptation to have sex as an act of rebellion against me.

Cynthia sat through this sermon so many times that eventually we got it boiled down to merely a hand signal indicating the number three and a facial expression that said, "Don't forget!" Cynthie's reply was a tightened jaw and rolled, closing eyes with a nod yes that pleaded, "I know, Mom; you don't have to tell me again."

From time to time, my daughter would come to me and ask me to shed more light on one or more of the Three Things. As long as she was asking, I kept my answers somewhat spare, encouraging her to ask more, which I'd then eagerly answer, acknowledging her for her clear thinking and insightful inquiry. During those years, I think Cynthia slept like a rock, dreaming of this fabulous experience awaiting her. But I stared at the ceiling much the same as I had done at Nancy Grady's house, back in Columbus, Ohio, in 1959.

Then came a few years during which the phone rang constantly and it was never for me. Photographs of hairless teenage boy bodies, ripped from magazines, began to clutter Cynthie's bedroom walls. Different boys' names were feverishly scrawled trillions of times on note pads, desk tops and woodwork. I took to calling Cynthia by the name Alice, short for, "One-a-these-days, Alice, BOOM! to the moon!" from *The Honeymooners*. This benign display of frustration generally dispersed the mother/daughter tension and kept us on an even keel.

Then came Russell. During one of Alice's visits back to the Midwest, her best girlfriend from grade school introduced her to Russell, a red-headed pink little dweeb with glasses and bad intentions. I loathed him from the start. But Alice (the teen formerly known as Cynthia) was enchanted, more with the notion of a love interest than with Russell specifically. I kept my opinion of Russell to myself, realizing I could only damage lines of communications with my young pistol of a daughter if I spoke up. And she continued to obsess about this geek in Indiana. I decided to react to the charm of her crush rather than the object of it.

Then suddenly, I started receiving colossal long distance phone bills for calls to Indianapolis. Alice didn't know the phone numbers she called would be listed, so she was incredulous when I went goose-stepping into her room and demanded to know whose phone number that was and how she intended to pay for all those calls. That first month, I educated her in the value of $120, the price of her passion, and warned her against doing that again. I gave her stationery and stamps, then I grounded her for two weeks for the crime of attempting to stiff her own Mom. But love triumphs over reason, especially when you're 14 and have no particular interest in reason.

Every month for an entire year, she called Russell to the tune of $100+ and charged it to me. When I finally realized that grounding her did nothing but further decay her attitude towards me, I forced her to sell her bicycle to pay back the debt. So she did, and promptly ran up more phone bills. I locked all the phones in a closet before I left the house and helped Alice get a telemarketing job that she could do in the evenings when I was at home. This way, she'd get sick of the telephone and earn enough to pay me back. She then simply charged her calls to Russell to my phone from her girlfriends' houses or from pay phones. In those days, there were no phone company services to help prevent her from doing this. So I honed my creative punishments and she declared an all-out war on me. And who better to listen to her plight but Russell? The plot thickened.

When summer came again and school let out, she asked me if she could go back to Indianapolis to see her girlfriend, and, of course, Prince Charming. I knew full well that it was my only chance to beat this long distance mess for a month, so I said yes.

"I think this year, Russell and I . . . are going to . . . you know . . . *do it.*"

With Alice's announcement, she held up three fingers to assure me she didn't need to hear the lecture again. I stared at her and sighed, and felt my face take that Mona Lisa shape. "Any questions?" I asked. "Not now, Mom. Maybe later." She then went next door to tell the neighbor girl that she was about to give it up to Russell. I went directly to the drugstore and bought a gross of condoms.

The night before her flight, I stuffed the condoms in every piece of clothing she had packed. They filled her shoes, bras and jeans pockets. They were between the pages of her book and in the bristles of her hairbrush. I also peppered her luggage with my business cards to remind her I'd be available for any necessary refresher courses.

I think I must've blacked out there for a while after she left for Indiana, because I cannot, for the life of me, remember the actual goodbye, or even the exact reason I decided to let her go in the first place. I only remember sitting on my waterbed and staring at the imported Indian bedspread for an eternity with my eyebrows pinched together. I was pretty sure life would never really be the same again.

Every time we spoke on the phone, I resisted asking Alice any prying questions about her love life. She said she was having fun with Russell and things were fine. She seemed to despise me much less than she had when she left, so I made every attempt to keep it that way.

At the conclusion of her visit, I picked Alice up at the airport, enjoying a heartfelt embrace and some giddy summer fun stories, spoken at teen warp-speed. I waited until the baggage claim signs were no longer visible in my rearview mirror before popping the question. "Well? Did you and Russell . . . you know, *do it?*" I said with all the nonchalance I could muster. "Y'know . . ." she replied very seriously, "I remembered what you told me about making my first time a sweet memory . . . and I decided not to do it, 'cause me 'n Russell weren't getting along *that* well. And I wanted to make sure the first time was great . . . like you said."

In my mind, I turned a cartwheel and came down in the splits, but what came out of my mouth was, "And how's your heart?" And Alice said her heart was fine. As I recall, the car was silent after that, and we drove home smiling proudly and looking straight ahead out the windshield.

In the movie, Claudia Larsen has a control-freak sister and a charmingly unstable gay brother. They all go to Baltimore for Thanksgiving. In my family, I have two straight brothers and the lion's share of neuroses myself. And Christmas is always a Pittsburgh break (if you can even fathom those two words together) from Mom and Dad's winter palace in Fort Lauderdale.

Home for the Holidays
A survivor's frightening account.

1989

It was the night before leaving for Pittsburgh, and Mom called to inform me that it was very cold there. I hid my shock well. After all, I lived in Boston and it *was* the end of November. I assured her I'd bring a coat. She told me she had called four times before and hung up when she heard "that answering machine pick up." In five weeks, it will be 1990 except at Mom and Dad's house, where 1956 will never end. Before she said "see you tomorrow," Dad interrupted to remind me to get to the airport half an hour before my flight. He said they would be waiting for me "with painted breath."

The next morning would begin the four hellish days

spent with my family. Ninety-six hours jam-packed with television, eating and being treated like an idiot.

I took a coat. Even though I'm 40 years old with a grown child of my own, I respond to these parental directives with the fevered "Awww, Jeez!" of a 15 year old. I had half a mind not to take a bloody coat. Whenever I deal with my parents, in fact, it's with half a mind. Good Lord, what kind of ignoramus do they take me for?! OK, OK: I should know better. But this problem doesn't reside in the domain of knowing. This one is in the gut, where only anti-anxietal drugs seem to help.

I envy people who enjoy the company of their parents without the aid of pharmaceuticals. Of course, my own daughter is among these folks, who share common interests, tastes and even a sense of humor with their parents. But for me, it's often a stiff regimen of meditation, hot baths, camomile tea, Excedrin and lots of counting to ten. And judging from the horror stories I've heard about other people's families, mine are *terrific parents*. They are, indeed, exceedingly good and well-intended people. Very well suited to attend to the needs of *small* children. If I were a perfect person, I would readily deem this far more important than these silly little gatherings at which they still consider me helpless without their guidance.

They're poor but generous. These folks won $500 in the lottery last Christmas and donated every last cent to a family who'd been burned out of their house. It shouldn't matter to me that they eat cheese that squirts out of a can. Or that they drone on and on about the obvious. These gripes I could perhaps keep to myself. And what better time than Thanksgiving to give it yet another try?

I sat on the Pittsburgh-bound plane, running familial drills in my head. I'll find absolutely nothing edible at their house. Mom will have stocked the place with sweets, unripened fruit, canned vegetables and squirt cheese. They'll act as though I'm being haughty for insisting on fresh vegetables and desserts without tons of sugar in them. I'll cook with fresh garlic. Mom will hold up a dusty container of garlic salt from 1956 and think I'm being snooty when I say, "No thanks, I don't mind chopping this." It'll be OK. I'll remind myself that if I don't act like it's a big deal, it'll just be a matter of grocery shopping and cooking for myself. I do that all the time.

They'll tell me I'm too skinny. They'll wonder if I'm anorexic or on chemotherapy. (Mom's hobby is illness and doom. There will be plenty of boil and hemorrhoid reports.) I will try to accept this as a primitive expression of the problem of mortality. After all, I share that problem.

Dad's hobby, creative worrying, would suck me into ridiculous conversations about terrorists, famine and compound fractures. I'll just reassure him, no matter what.

The bed pillows will be like foam rubber surf-boards. That's OK, because I've packed my own pillow. Everything will have an artificial pine or lemon scent from some toxic product. It won't kill me in just five days. I'll roll with it. A frenzied eating will occur about every 40 minutes. Hey, everybody chooses their own poison. I'll leave them alone about the smoking and the squirt cheese. Andy Williams will bellow Christmas songs from the 1956 hi-fi while Dad watches the news. Over all this, my parents will conduct a full-volume conversation from different rooms. And I will be *patient*.

(Patient:, adj. Bearing pains or trials calmly or without complaint. Manifesting forbearance under provocation or strain.
Not hasty or impetuous. Steadfast despite opposition, difficulty or adversity.)

They'll do the things they've always done to drive me nuts and I won't go nuts. I'll translate every single thing into a gesture of love and concern. These are two things of which I'm certain. This time, I will exhibit a mastery over the situation. My hard-earned maturity will bridge the abyss. Yep. It's going to be great.

An awful panic overtook me at 22,000 feet. I should've never started down Memory Lane, for many more land mines awaited me than just the aforementioned. Once this list-making began, I couldn't stop it. And my resolve to handle this mounting litany of predictable torments began to shimmy but good.

Dad, the retired airplane mechanic, will take another crack at offering me advice about my business, which is writing. (Mind you, this is the guy with "painted breath.") They'd want to know if I'm any closer to being married and thereby resembling the picture they'd hoped I'd grow into. And Mom will beat me at Scrabble and then rub it in. They'll mispronounce words. Mom will take her clothes off in front of me at least once. Horrible, grueling, unnecessary tidbits will be discussed at great length. I will have to learn about at least one amputation. Long-winded, bizarre theories about stupid things will rake my nerves. They won't understand why I dress this way. Mom will talk through her nose.

Oh, God. We're landing.

The airline lost my coat. I had put the very coat I had assured my Mother I'd bring into a drawstring bag and checked it with my baggage. The drawstring bag went somewhere else for Thanksgiving. I look like a local girl in Mom's dorky coat. I'm already over the edge. I've been on the ground 30 minutes.

The first of the bizarre theories came from Mom. She couldn't imagine that USAir would lose *one* of my bags and not *the other one*. I pointed out that they didn't keep people's luggage together by name tags and that this was entirely plausible. Only 95 hours to go, I thought.

On the way home in the car, Dad was so busy with the harmony part to the song playing on the all-50's station that he took a curve too fast and the bag of donuts slid across the dash. Mom registered a near-death experience and criticized his driving. He muttered something about not using enough rudder. He pointed out a building where he had once had two teeth extracted. And Mom described a disgusting seeping fungus their dog had in his ears. Never mind that Bunky has been dead for years.

"Uncle Freddy is a great guy, but he farts when he walks," Dad said. There is no way to offer repartee in the face of this verbal buckshot. I'm simply not clever enough. I must've seemed to be quite dull to them, staring out the window with my mouth dropped open slightly. Already defeated. Wearing Mom's coat.

My assimilation into their home life continued from there. And so did the riveting conversation. Mom actually read me a form letter from their insurance company. Dad reminded me again that *all* the women on his side of the family had eventually developed Alzheimer's disease and were full-fledged legumes before signing off.

Then he played "Dark Town Strutter's Ball" and "Anchors Aweigh" on the organ. (Melody only.) And with the aid of that foot pedal, he created the sense that the Wurlitzer was actually lunging toward you and then recoiling only to come for you again and again. This menacing effect added an hallucinogenic quality to the gathering which didn't seem to bother anyone else.

I fled to the upstairs bathroom where my suspicions were confirmed. I had gotten a nosebleed. It's a wonder that's the only thing that ruptured.

Just as I was plotting a phony illness and an

emergency escape back to Boston, a reprieve came along. NBA basketball. Channel seven. I convinced them to stop playing music and just watch the game. We snuggled right into a common interest. Mom criticized the Knicks' defense and a chorus of "Oh!s" and "Yes!s" began to remind us of our bond. Dad grumbled that "Stuffing the ball was no god-damned talent. W'hell, if you're 6'11", *'course* you can slam it in—but that's not basketball!" And our traditional arguing ensued.

I employed the drills I had run on the airplane and changed the subject in a sudden burst of diplomacy. "How about some Scrabble, Mom?" Well, I hadn't seen Mom move that fast in a long time. "You bet," she said with victory in her voice.

While we played, Dad loped out into the kitchen and dished up some pecan pie with whipped cream and a coke, sat down at the Wurlitzer and played "Roll Out the Barrel" while the *Tonight Show* theme song blared in the background. Then he took an applauseless bow and decided to spray the carpet with lemon scented anti-static stuff from an aerosol can. He sat down in a fog of that stuff and ate his pie. Mom kicked my ass at Scrabble.

Within this short time, I had resigned myself to somnambulating through the remaining visit, in the name of duty and gratitude. (And yes, Thanksgiving.) I didn't think they would notice. We were all three dead on our feet now. The Zombie Family Reunion.

Without a reference point to the life I live when *I* have something to say about it, I sank into a withdrawn haze and began to think more and more about snacking. I reassured myself that I could resist the squirt cheese. (I have only a matter of hours to go.) I knew it was time to resort to a sure-fire distraction. Old photos.

Among them, I found pictures of my paternal grandmother, my father and both brothers posing with their respective basketball teams. And zillions of pictures from the '50s, when my parents were still geniuses in my eyes. They were the ones with The Answers. No empty banter back then. Their vast knowledge impressed me for many years. My respect for them was repaid with what seemed then to be an unconditional love. I saw myself reflected in my parents' eyes with a golden glow over me. (The very same strength in my specialness that later led me to break rules, become opinionated and set myself apart from others.)

Those were happy times before the deafening clash of ideology. Before I could be criticized for being single. When I ate what was squirted in front of me. And before the *globe*.

Grandpa gave me the whole world back in '56. He had no idea that he would forever disrupt the ignorant bliss that had kept our family a unit until then. I *loved* that globe. I felt a certain reverence for the plastic ball, thinking I'd never been that close to the whole world before, and now it was mine. I remember my father pointing with a darning needle to a spot near the middle of North America, and saying, "There's Columbus, Ohio—this is where you are *right now*." I can't express how thrilled I was by this. Because that meant that no matter where I looked on my globe, there was somebody there, *right now,* too. I tried to picture them, so I could fill my whole world up with the appropriate people in the right place *right then.*

This led to a series of questions about other people in the world that marked the end of my parents' genius. Up to that point, Dad was an authority on aerodynamics and clouds. Mom knew the names of really fancy diseases and could spell anything. They could identify any animal and tap dance adequately around tougher questions. But right then, my world got bigger than theirs. And I developed a preoccupation with the fleeting consecutive "nows" that passed in distant places without my experience of them. I plotted to replace the sacrificed contentment of home with my very own big world.

Que sera, sera. Dad was pouting. I could even tell when he was chewing that pecan pie. He went down into the basement where his all-50's radio was blaring, to work on another of his primitive wire airplane sculptures. When he didn't sing along with Doris Day to "Que Sera, Sera," I knew he was really steamed about something. It was me. I had declined their invitation to go to church, which they insisted would be entirely up to me. I opted to stay home and watch the national news and try to remember who I was. When I asked Mom why Dad was acting that way, she lied and said he was pissed at *her.* But I knew she was just trying to prevent a confrontation, a long-standing tradition in my family, often conducted with the Up with People Singers in the background.

So as soon as Mom skunked me in Scrabble, I took a boiling bath and a Valium to prepare for the following day. And don't you know, USAir delivered the missing bag with my coat in it just then. I looked at it with a weird jealousy before opening it, wondering where in the big world it had gone without me.

Ho Boy. Grazing began extra early on Thanksgiving morning. My brothers arrived with assorted girlfriends, wives and children. And there were fried eggs, pancakes, "crew-sonts," fudge, cookies, sticks of butter disguised as every manner of food. Mom made us go look at the long icicles coming off the corners of the shed. The kids bounced up and down. Dad recited in-flight emergency procedures. And on TV, the Johnny Mann Singers sang "Y'gotta have heart," as only they can. Dad repeated his complaint about Uncle Freddy repeating his stories. Mom told everyone about the oozing lesion of somebody we didn't know. The question "Is Disneyland more fun than Busch Gardens?" was tossed out for debate. Dad went outside to look at the sky and missed Mom's brief history of nasty gashes suffered in our family.

Mom and Dad lumbered about the house, all swollen, like bloated ghosts, chewing as they walked. It was the Macy's Parade of Parents. People cordially offered each other another appetizer. Bizarre theories about things flew. Dad speculated that the airport would be busy again soon because people don't get Friday off.

Thanksgiving breakfast just sort of blended into lunch, which turned into a crescendo of dinner, followed by a deafening silence.

Casualties of the meal sprawled out in various unlovely positions in front of the TV, horrified at what we had just eaten. And the only thanks I could think of was, "Thank God it isn't Christmas." Because Christmas is the same scene, *plus* gift-giving and receiving, the dramatization of which is an exhausting undertaking. In my family, believe me, it is far, far better to give than to receive.

Last year, I received a size 18/20 dress from one of my brothers, who's "born again" (making him my youngest brother, I guess), and who hadn't seen me in two years and figured I'd probably doubled in size like most Radants do. He also tossed in a stocking stuffer inspirational cassette tape, the cover of which reads, "No matter your age, the approval of your parents affects how you view yourself and your ability to pass that approval along to your children. Many people spend a lifetime looking for this acceptance the Bible calls The Blessing." All year, I felt just a little bit suspicious about that gift. Like, what was he trying to say? I always felt blessed by our folks—does he know something I don't?

My niece and nephew gave me a perfectly nice black sweatshirt, onto which they had applied some sort of clumpy paint substance in a random design. I finally got it scraped off with a razor blade so I could wear it to the gym.

Mom and Dad, defeated from years of giving gifts I obviously hated, asked me to buy my own damned presents last year. They gave me $100 and told me to go wild. I did.

And the one brother I can easily relate to . . . the one who arrived in 1962, years after the globe . . . the baby I sang to and kissed until he fell asleep, this one brother who *knows me,* gave me a watch with a hologram of a globe on the crystal. That was a wonderful Christmas.

* * *

Mom's voice broke the silence with an offer no one could refuse. A round of Alka-Seltzers. And a thunderous fizzing ensued.

Later that night, I creamed Mom at Scrabble. After everyone left, I cleared the table, examining bowl after bowl of the food, which had cooled to a consistency of Jell-O infused with tub and tile caulking. It wobbled. I stood there for a moment, realizing that this is the stuff my parents are made of and that's why they wobbled in the same fashion. I looked up at both of them for a comparison and found them looking back at me, puzzled that I was standing there shaking bowls of food with that look on my face.

Then we went out to see a movie about airplanes that Dad wanted to see. I heard him muttering to the screen to "keep the nose up . . . air speed's too low. . . ." On the way home, Dad worried that I might, someday, for some reason, be taken hostage.

Mom squirmed in the front seat to show me where her back hurt. And finally, back at home, I trounced my Mother at her own game. Crushed her by a healthy 120-point spread and declared that I would never play Scrabble with her again so that my triumph would stand. She congratulated me and told me that Mike Nolan had died mercilessly of a horrible brain tumor.

They took me to the airport the next day. I wore my own coat and my hologram globe watch from last Christmas. Dad was concerned about the plane I was taking back to Boston and about the possibility of another ice age. Mom reminded me to tip the porter and check the monitor to find out what gate to go to. I kissed them goodbye and walked towards the terminal door. I resisted turning a series of cartwheels and paused to wave farewell before disappearing into the airport. Any minute now, the big world would be mine again.

I looked into their eyes and saw myself again with that golden light all over me. They never understood my alternative ways and yet they've tolerated me all this time. I saw how much they missed being geniuses. My heroes.

Growing up in my family, there was no such thing as abundance. We had everything we needed and Dad made the rest out of scrap lumber and duct tape. So somewhere along the line, I decided that whenever I got that vague, uncomfortable feeling like I needed something, I automatically assumed it was one of those things we never had at home. I was correct about 15% of the time. The rest is yard sale history.

The Boston Phoenix, *recognizing my authority on the topic, published this story in their May 3, 1991, issue.*

Retail therapy
The sick way to feel better fast.

1991

Okay, so times get tight. Witness the post-'80s reality check of the 1990–1992 recession.

Off and on, you hear the whining of newly humbled homeowners who are suffering through, cutting corners on debauchery and having to skip this year's spa vacation. But for many people, financial security is a tidal kind of thing. It comes and it goes with a predictable, often dreadful regularity.

Take my case, for instance. I live in the exciting and ever-changing world of the freelance writer, where a person can make literally hundreds and hundreds of dollars producing articles just like this one. When I'm *really* feeling ambitious (or when the landlord shows his fangs) I have the option of bagging the nonlucrative domain of speaking my mind and selling *more expensive, less heartfelt* words to advertising folks.

This dilemma—the cavernous difference between what I want to do and what I have to do—fairly drives me bonkers. And I'm in plenty of good company. (You have probably noticed all the other crazy people around.) In fact, I'll bet this is the leading cause of weirdness in folks these days.

Now, since a bonkers freelance writer who's careening willy-nilly towards bankruptcy really has *no business* undertaking a topic as large as *The Leading Cause of Weirdness in Western Civilization Today,* I would like to focus instead on just *one* of the mysterious behaviors therein. I call it *Poverspending Gravis*— a grave case of overspending in the face of abject poverty.

Poverspending Gravis is a gross overreaction to having no spending money and feeling you deserve better. It's the crippling urge to toss reason to the wind and charge what should be rightfully yours. An optimist might call it a law-abiding substitute for stealing. A fatalist would say it's a dark destiny, self-fulfilled. A realist might say it's plain old sad. And when I get some dough together, I'll let you know what my therapist calls it.

"It" happened just the other day. Let's just say I was "between hundreds" when I was taken by this irrepressible hunger for a nice salade niçoise, an expensive glass of white burgundy, and the pretense that it was all a treat from American Express, in thanks for my years of financial slavery. I enjoyed this little fantasy *so* much, I then decided to see what Mr. Bloomingdale would like to do in my honor. It all happened so *fast*.

Literally hundreds and *hundreds* of dollars later, I returned to my humble abode with a wine headache and a sense of deep shame. "Crap!" I thought, wearing my new *Paris* cologne, "What a bonehead thing to do." And as I slinked past the mirror in my foyer, I saw a pouting woman whose lips were a smashing shade of Lancôme's Loudest Red, wearing a new Todd Oldham dress and a dunce cap. "*Now* I'm going to have to write a small-space ad for sleep sofas, a brochure about prosciutto, and that piece about the Sheraton in Shanghai to make up for this!"

For me, writing advertising copy is the only fast-acting antidote to *Poverspending Gravis*. And this was a textbook case.

A small consolation was that I knew I wasn't the first woman in the world to shop in the face of deprivation . . . to shake my fist at adversity . . . to roll up my Adrienne Vittadini sleeves and purchase again, against all reason. But why? I plugged in my new digital alarm clock, took one lap around the house with my new four-horsepower Hoover, and sat down over a cup of fresh-ground Kona coffee and tried to figure out just exactly what had happened to me. After several high-octane cups of Kona and exactly 54 minutes of fruitless puzzling, I gave myself a facial and went to bed.

A few days later, when I told my girlfriend Marie about this little glitch in my good judgment, she told me about a similar time in her life when she found herself, broke and grumbling, shuffling down a grey New York City street towards her tiny condo when she spotted "the shoes of (her) dreams" in a store window. "They were only a half size too small, so I got them in three colors," she said. We exchanged a high five and agreed we were both idiots.

Then I remembered the time back in 1988 when my buddy Paula called and acted a little funny, like she had something on her mind, but couldn't quite get it out. We discussed topics we normally don't. Until finally she cut to the chase. "Let me ask you a weird question . . ." she said with a nervous giggle. ". . . Do you, by any chance, need any Tupperware?"

Now I knew Paula was hurting for money, but I couldn't feature her moonlighting as a Tupperware salesperson. "*Tupperware?*" I said incredulously. And she burst into tears.

Seems Paula had been stricken by the same urges Marie and I had been, only the poor dear found herself trapped at a Tupperware party at the time of her brave rebellion against poverty. She ordered a whopping $500 worth of tubs, trinkets and burping containers. Now she had to try to redeem herself by reselling some of it to her friends. I got off easy, with only a celery crisper and a sandwich-shaped tub. I think she also unloaded a salt and pepper set on someone and gave the rest away as gifts for the next several Christmases. She will never live it down.

But when it comes to this Poverspending Gravis affliction, no one can compare to my friend Lilly. Here is a black belt connoisseur whose income will never *ever* shake hands with her spending. Lilly is a threat to any single man who's sacrificed, climbed the ladder of success and worked weekends to get ahead. She is the destroyer of all savings, a savage, single-minded shopper who always gets her merchandise. She belongs in the Shopping Steamrollers' Hall of Shame.

I met this charming and dangerous woman soon after moving to Boston to get my kid in the best public school in America. We made plans to meet in the Faneuil Hall rotunda for lunch. The only thing I really knew about Lilly at that point was that she was likely to be late. So I wore my Walkman and leaned up against a pole to indulge in crowd observation until I saw her brown eyes off in the distance, parting the throngs like Moses at the Red Sea. Her jaw was set and she approached mē urgently and grabbed both of my forearms as she spoke.

"I got my bill consolidation loan," she said with a sparkle. And I was so swept up with her glee that I offered to buy us a bottle of champagne to celebrate. She guided me directly to the most expensive bottle of hooch I'd ever seen. We popped the cork out into the Boston Harbor and sat on a seaside bench, giggling and drinking lunch. This inaugurated a long and pricey relationship the likes of which I had never known before.

Up until I met Lilly, I didn't know how much I needed certain luxuries in my own life. I owe many of the comforts I now enjoy to her earlier influence. Together, we owe *bundles* to every company supplying plastic cards.

I will never forget when Lilly, surrounded by the prospect of financial ruin and irrevocably tethered to a life of debt, called two of her brothers, borrowed money from each of them, and then flew to New York for the weekend. When she came home, she was wearing an expensive pair of royal blue Italian shoes and a Cheshire cat smile. I was awestruck.

Thank heaven, Lilly has since moved to California, where she can do far less harm to my future and the future of my descendants. I miss spending the big bucks with her something awful, but I take comfort in the notion that without her high-falutin' tastes here on the East Coast, I can afford the occasional airplane ticket to go visit her.

* * *

Poverspending Gravis is a bizarre phenomenon and our culture is steeped in it. It is the counter-melody to "America the Beautiful"; sort of a Kurt Weill anthem of western civilization, the tune to which ruthless consumers, in the throes of economic strain, continue to charge on—to the death.

But even though I've compiled and participated in these case studies, I'm afraid that the behavior remains a mystery. I only know it hits hardest in the demography of those who have, once upon a time, tasted forbidden designer fruit. Innocent children never display this strange behavior, but learn quickly from their parents. And men react quite differently to the syndrome from how we women do. Their coping rituals tend more to involve either cars, beer, or women wearing clothes we can't afford.

Poverspending Gravis is so peculiarly American that I think I'll attempt to declare this most recent "outburst" of mine a tax deduction. After all, by writing this article, I've turned my affliction into (easily a hundred dollars' worth of) income.

And speaking of income, it's redemption time. Back to the real-life, make-a-buck world of advertising for me. My Monday morning deadline on the Sheraton job is fast approaching. Let's see . . .

"Enjoy the best of the Western world in the heart of ancient China. The Shanghai Sheraton is convenient to the city's best restaurants and a dizzying array of shopping pleasures."

I should be locked away.

Former spring chicken
tells all
What it's like to career into middle age.

1994

Picture this: *Leggy, lanky babe with long blond hair serves a short sentence in maternity clothes, goes to art school, models, figures out how to provide for offspring and grows up. (In that order.) Later packs up teenaged daughter and moves from Cincinnati to Brookline for its renowned school system.* That babe was me. And by the time I hit my thirties, there was no freak-out about my age. I was thrilled to have a jump-start on my girlfriends, whose clocks were beginning to tick loudly. The only fertility worry *I* had was my daughter's. Boston University students would hoot and make animal noises when I walked down the street, and I'd act indignant and think, "Chill out, buddy-boy, I'm old enough to be your mother," loving every minute of it. I always looked younger than my age.

On my 40th birthday, my girlfriend Louise and I went to the beach where she took pictures of me in a bathing suit. (Now I won't even wear one.) When I was 41 people in boutiques where my 22-year-old daughter and I shopped blanched when she called me Mom. Neither Louise, a former state champion swimmer and all-around jock, nor my young daughter could keep up with me in aerobics class. I was genetically blessed, athletically inclined and a serial optimist. When it came to aging, I couldn't figure what all the fuss was about. Deep down, I *really* believed it would never happen to me.

Well, it happened. Not overnight, not even over the course of a few months. But somewhere between my 40th birthday and today, I have been stricken with the sudden onset of aging. The years of ballet, softball, jogging and high-impact aerobics are finally palpable in my joints. I see a perceptible drop in the jowls, the eyelids and the skin above my knees. And I've started craving naps. All of this has been subtle. I know the awareness of it has crept upon me before anyone else can notice. Except for the weight gain.

But before I tell that part, you must picture this: *In 1989, at the peak of my cardiovascular fitness—at the pinnacle of my self-possession, a terrible mishap in a dentist's chair leaves me with the kind of injury that would make an emergency room nurse cringe. It is worse than the scene in* Marathon Man. I was in pain for two whole years with something called necrosis of the bone. I couldn't say words like necrosis, though, because putting my teeth together to say the S's made me shudder with pain. I became very quiet, extremely weak and non-athletic, because physical activity increased the throbbing in my face. Transformed into such a different kind of person, I also became depressed. Looking back on that time now, it seems clear to me that this episode marked the beginning of the end of my youth. The only saving grace was that since I couldn't eat, I became very thin. And we all know what a crowd-pleaser thin is. So until I finally became absolutely skeletal, people were continually telling me I looked great.

After all the bone tissue died and some soft tissue regenerated over the exposed nerve endings, the pain finally subsided. There was a brief but blissful time when I could enjoy food again and I didn't gain weight. As luck would have it, I was working (as travel advance person for the Stones) in Europe at the time, and dining in some of the finest restaurants. My job required me to walk all over 26 major European cities, which, along with the rigors of travel, kept me lean. When I returned to the States, though, my DNA seemed to remember who I was and I slowly, steadily, turned Rubenesque, as B.U. students passed by in silence.

First, I noticed some of my clothes were tight, but I shrugged it off, thinking I must've gotten them during my ultra-skinny days after the dentistry accident. Then I detected a sort of a ricochet when I walked . . . a boogedy-boogedy butt-echo that I found highly unpleasant. It was almost as if someone were following me. So, acting as my former long, lanky self, I took matters in hand and began running—literally trying to run my butt off. It was January and I went to visit my daughter in the Union of South Africa, where she had set up home with her South African boyfriend. It was mid-summer. While she and her friends would congregate in the evenings to smoke cigarettes and drink a few beers with dinner, I'd go off for a run.

Picture it: *A tall, strapping midwestern blonde charging down the streets of Johannesburg, smiling and chirping "Hello!" to the Zulus heading back to the homelands after work.* During that month in Africa, my kid, her boyfriend and I took a trip south and stayed in a campground on the Indian Ocean. The "youngsters" went off on what I feared would be a booze cruise, so I opted to spend the evening alone at our hut. I read, napped and decided to time my evening run with the breathtaking sunset that was just starting to pinken the African sky. The campsite was situated at the base of a splendid mountain that I could run up. (Remember the Olympic trainees from Africa who ran up mountains? I drew no significant distinction between them and myself at that stage.) So I chugged skyward up that mountain until the sunset was peaking, then turned and descended, full-throttle, with my favorite music on the Walkman and a roaring runner's rush. It was like flying. I just feasted my eyes on the Indian Ocean below and the sunset that completely encircled me. An ostrich glanced my way from afar. I was in heaven.

At around 3:00 the following morning, I awoke with a pain in my hip joint that was so intense it felt like I was being stabbed. It wasn't a tribal attack. It was bursitis. A year and a half later, I still have a bum hip and a good story to tell about it. And I realize that in a matter of years, I will have enough injuries, aches and pains to bore the pants off people. "Yes, Chris, you've *told* us the story about running down a mountain in Africa." That's the kind of stuff old ladies cluck to each other about. That and their grandchildren and their friends who drop dead one after another.

> *"The great quest awaits us all. We may ignore or resist it, but none of us can avoid it. Some deal with the mid-life quest in their thirties and others deny it well into senescence. But no matter where you are now, know that getting old turns out to have less to do with physical appearance than with fear and truth; and less to do with death than with the true meaning of life."*

Someone named Marsden Freed wrote this, and a buddy of mine cut it out of a brochure and placed it between a magnet and her refrigerator. I saw it there just before my 44th birthday.

I'm not sure who this Freed flunky is, but the fact of the matter is that aging (*"the quest"*) sucks. It creates a sudden segregation between you and the body you've always considered to be you. The first reaction is to look down at the damn thing and wonder, "Hey! What'd I ever do to *you?*" (I know, I know. Single parenthood, high-stress jobs, high-impact aerobics, that mountain in Africa . . .) And you begin to think of yourself and of the body that's disobeying you in separate terms.

For me, the logical first step was to go to a body specialist to see about correcting these body things. The doctor learned I was hypothyroid, a common thyroid imbalance that often accounts for weight gain and sudden-onset napping. I encouraged him to just go wild with his synthroid prescription. "I won't mind if my eyes bug out a bit, just make me lanky again," I told him. But no such luck. My thyroid levels returned to normal without bringing my self-image with them. I made a second trip to the doctor to demand an explanation and possibly even plead for some sort of reductive surgery. He sent me to a nutritionist in the Cardiac Risk Unit. (Cardiac Risk? Oh yeah; my Mom's whole family went down to heart disease . . .)

In the midst of all this, I visited a friend my age and complained about my body, which, in my view, had reached maximum density. "The jeans that were just tight enough to make me cranky before now won't zip shut!" I tell her with a St. Bernard face.

Without a word, my girlfriend smiled, left the room and returned with Gail Sheehy's book about menopause.

"Menopause!?" I gasped at my friend, "Whose side are you on?"

I opened it at random and read a few sentences under a subhead that read "Cinderella hits menopause." I read a paragraph describing the author's trip to California to attend a discussion group on the topic. "Going to Hollywood to talk about menopause," she wrote, "was a bit like going to Las Vegas to sell savings accounts." And since I happen to share Hollywood's view that menopause is a terminal disease, I asked to borrow the book.

Back to the doctor, who by now must've been considering a psych referral. My hormone levels indicated no onset of menopause yet. But by now, I'd read the book and understood why women *don't* talk about the bleak prospects that await us all. Picture Marlon Brando in the final scene of *Apocalypse Now,* saying "The horror . . . the *horror!*"

By then, I was fully engaged in an age obsession. Louise gave me a copy of *Longevity* magazine, chocked cover-to-cover with ads and articles about younger-looking skin, vitamins that keep you smarter, stronger and healthier longer, yoga postures and aromatherapies. I bought skin-tightening beauty concoctions with four-page instruction booklets. Blew the dust off my abdomenizer. Sent for information from the Hemlock Society. And then, God help me, I joined a gym.

I had only two criteria: The gym had to be close to home and it couldn't be one of those spandex-y thong places where people join in order to meet hunks and babes. And bingo! Vinny Greco's Powerhouse Gym, a 10-minute walk from my house, fit the bill. But picture this: *Aging female athlete limps into gym followed by her ricocheting butt, wearing running skins and (the dead giveaway) oversized T-shirt*. It took some nerve to sashay through the foreign pieces of metal and the clusters of bulging, straining body builders half my age. Because I could see myself through their eyes and I looked like I was in the wrong building.

Sprawling the entire length and breadth of a second-story warehouse, Vinny Greco's was unlike any gym or dance studio I'd ever frequented. It looked like the structural ruins of some secret society. Dull silver contraptions with massive black disks and stacks of brick-like weights that clank when they meet. Portraits of bodybuilders hung on the walls, signed with nicknames like "Quadzilla." All around were bronzed, grimacing weight lifters with baseball hats on backwards and every manner of odd belt, gloves and straps. They had arms like the sleeves of Ricky Ricardo's Babaloo shirts, and they slurped neon-colored god-knows-what. They sat on stationary bikes reading muscle magazines full of words like *ripped, cut, buff* and *anabolic*. They generated colossal puddles of sweat. A few of them congregated at the juice bar to discuss amino acids over snacks of nuked egg whites and plain tuna. The truth is that on that first day, many of them frightened me a little when I imagined my daughter roaming the same streets they do. But I braced myself and focused on the familiar smell of effort and the somewhat common purpose.

By the end of my first training session, though, I had discovered the perfectly accessible and yes, *gentle* cores of several of the Michelin men. They were not the guys out boosting cars and bothering people. In fact, I quickly got the impression that their bulk was intended to act as a silent statement to others to please just leave them alone. They encouraged me, didn't mock me and we all went about our business. Plus I practically had the women's locker room to myself.

One evening last fall after a long workout, I was camped in front of the TV, rubbing my aching calves, waiting for the sloughing agent on my face to dry, paging through a Covert Bailey book and slurping a neon-colored god-knows-what. And synchronicity served me up a very effective reality check: I heard the TV announcer say, "Have you noticed your daughter obsessing about diet, exercising constantly and having a poor self-image? Learn the signs of anorexia and bulimia. Watch our special, Thursday night, and you could save your daughter's life."

I became furious. Society *loves* the way starving women look! Why the hell else would I have spent the last two months chronicling every morsel I ate and working like a suffering dog at Vinny Greco's?

Just then the phone rang and my friend invited me to see the Rubens exhibition at the Museum of Fine Arts. I short-circuited. The women that Rubens painted were just regular women, shaped the way we women are programmed to be shaped. *I* didn't invent the soft, plush tummy, abundant bosom, or the boogedy-boogedy butt!

I realized just then that I had set out to fight the forces of nature and trick myself and everyone else into thinking that I was something entirely opposite to my strong, maternal, soft self. Like some pathetic balding guy who wears a convincing toupée but wonders when a wind would kick up and everyone would discover the ugly truth.

It was at that moment, before I could say, "Yeah, I'd love to see Rubens . . ." that I realized that I no longer *had* a desire to be the size of an insect or to dress like a slut. That I was *much* more than my dress size. That my friends and, even more surprisingly, my devoted boyfriend Dio love me for a litany of reasons that would stretch several pages before it got to "good measurements." And that maybe that's why the Zulus in Johannesburg looked so puzzled.

The word "jeepers" fell out of my mouth. My friend on the phone said, "Did you just say *jeepers?*" "Yeah, I'd love to see Rubens," I said and hung up. I was thunderstruck. That Marsden Freed guy is *not* a flunky. Aging does suck, but it forces an important lesson upon us. I'm not going to try to tell you what that lesson is, because you won't get it. You'll have to fly to Africa, build some biceps, cry in your pillow— and have your own damn crisis to figure it out.

Considering I didn't know yesterday what I know today about slipping into middle age, it's easy to see why it's so annoying and isolating to be surrounded by younger people (even a few years younger!) who don't know the first thing about it. They're just like I was, saying, "What's all the fuss about?" and secretly believing it won't happen to them. I realize I owe it to my daughter to accept this quest with some sanity and grace.

Now picture this: *After two months of hard work at Vinny Greco's, several doctor's visits, and some guidance from a crack nutritionist, I adjust my expectations. I do not expect to go the way of Jane Fonda. I have far too many other things to do in my life. But tempered by regular exercise, low fat intake and a policy of mental non-violence to myself, even a fraction of what I afford total strangers, I expect to do just exactly what aging female humans do: soften and sag, grow wise, wither and die.*

Having said that, I'm pleased to report that in these two months, I have lost 2¾" from my waist, 2" of bootie, and my bras fit me again. I've come to think of my workouts *not* as my ticket to transformation into Tinkerbell, but as something I can consider just another part of my daily ritual, like brushing my hair. I must maintain this over the long haul. Right around the time this dawned on me, I noticed the *other* people who belong to my gym. The handful of people my age, the doctors, firemen, moms and grandmoms, and very tubular, unpumped, regular robust people like me. Although I waver sometimes, I'm generally somewhere on that narrow path toward self-acceptance, moving away from the obsession to conform to this lean little flash in society's Teflon pan. No matter how I might still gripe about it, I now know the score.

Could this be maturity? Nah, I'm too young for that. Must be a hormonal swing.

Who do I think I am?
(And who are all these *other* people?)

1993

I must know two dozen people who, for one reason or another, have up-and-decided to change their names. This trend has rifled through my circle of friends and acquaintances like an influenza, and each time I learn of another new moniker, I get just a smidge more irritated.

Why should I have a problem with this? The ugly truth is that I believe myself to be the sole arbiter of taste in this department, sanctioning some changes and pooh-poohing others. Obviously, there *are* occasions for which a name change is necessary, such as in the case of Songbird, who became Robin, and Walter, who became Jeff. It's the people who've undergone *elective* name changes—those capricious imps who've simply decided to spice things up a bit—who really get under my skin. Frankly, I don't think they give a hoot about the trouble it puts the rest of us to. The Rolodex cards, party introductions and general alienation, for starters. And it's a good two to three years before the feeling of idiocy wears off when we try to say the new name with straight faces.

The very first person to try this idea out on me was my lovely daughter, Cynthia. I remember a rather grand entrance into our kitchen one day when she was all of seven, followed by an announcement that, "From now on, I would like to be called Vickie." With a deadpan face and a pointing index finger, I replied, "Got it, Vickie." I hadn't the slightest intention of following through, because I knew that by noon the next day she would be an astronaut or a pot of daisies. This is forgivable in pre-adolescence.

Later, when we were living in Ohio, where a Midwestern girl hankers to be more, I caught wind of someone named Marsha Schwartz, or something regular like that. The rumor goes that following some plastic surgery, she changed her name to Magna Frill and moved to California to seek her fortune. And apparently it *worked!* Word flew around Cincinnati that Magna had last been sighted skiing with the Hemingway girls and being quite fabulous. Hey, it beats busing tables at Denny's.

Then a blues and soul singer friend of mine who was christened "Barbara" switched to "Billie" in order to fit her stage image. We all took to it right away. After all, if you can sing well enough, people will call you anything you like.

But what about changing from Penny to Kate? Bill to William? Mary to Molly? OK, the latter in these three sets of names each has a different feel. Kate sounds more sturdy and in-charge than Penny. William is a grown-up's name and not so clipped and familiar as Bill. Molly is the name of a woman who's probably a good vegetarian cook, while Mary has most likely destroyed her self-esteem in parochial schools. So despite the inconvenience to me, Christine Radant, I can, after a period of clumsiness and resentment, get behind these name changes too.

But here's one that sent me into a snit: When Sandra changed to Artemis because she identified with the energy of the goddess of the same name. New age names are the absolute worst. These modern-day "re-creations" are, in my omnipresent opinion, fooling themselves and attempting to have the rest of us play along.

I remember the day of Sandra's big announcement. We were eating burritos and she was telling me about her trip to New Mexico. I should've seen it coming. She had already considered joining a coven and begun to call herself an artist almost immediately after her departure from her computer consultant job. So she says with a casual lilt, "Oh, did I tell you I changed my name to Artemis?" I swear the mariachi tape stopped playing and all I could hear was the voice in my head saying, "Right, and I'm Lefty the Wonder Dog, though I appear to be a Midwesterner with unruly hair. Honor me."

"Artemis?" I said with my eyebrows millimeters from my hairline. And she nodded yes.

This thing stuck in my craw for weeks. I couldn't bring myself to say it, for fear the "Lefty" association would spill out right behind. I toyed with calling her Art, then dismissed the idea as foolish. So I told the truth to Sandra. "I feel stupid calling you Artemis, and besides, the name doesn't conjure up an image of the daughter of Zeus, sister of Apollo, it makes me think of Artemus Gordon, that guy who played a cowboy in the '60s TV series, *The Wild, Wild West.*" And with that, our friendship was interrupted for many, many months.

So what's the problem here? Clearly, I am the problem. People most certainly have the right to change their names. In fact, I feel change should be mandatory for any former child named after a weather pattern, fungus or type of fabric. The real problem is snooty, opinionated people like me.

I can only hope that the next big trend will *not* be to call people by the names of their worst traits. "Jerk Radant" is a pathetic name for somebody's mother.

How one Radant got from 16th century France to Boston, Massachusetts, is a long, confusing story. What's really amazing is that it's me. Winter suits me for about a month and then I start wigging out.

Cabin fever

The effects of Boston winters on one woman's mood.

1993

A traditional New England winter takes a toll on one's self-esteem and general good cheer. Take me, for instance. As a freelance writer, I'm no stranger to staying home and wearing pajamas for days at a stretch. But even I have difficulty surviving the long dark months here in the upper right corner of our continent.

During this last siege of arctic air, I vowed I would not leave the house until the temperature rose to a balmy 32° or my nose stopped dripping, whichever came first. Today makes day five of my confinement and I'm nearing my limit, with no cessation of mucus in sight.

Odd, isn't it, that this is the season so often depicted in a romantic fashion on postcards of New England. The truth is, it brings out the absolute worst in people, making it easy to become both physically and temperamentally ugly. Oh, sure, *some* people love it. Every year, I hear some rosy-cheeked freak claim he stood by all summer long with his cross-country skis ready. This type of person perks right up during the unnerving stretch between Thanksgiving and New Year's, with hopes of snow flurries that would, in their warped perspective, add just the right holiday atmosphere to a season which to my mind is already marred by group activities and alcohol. I know these "winter people" exist, but I'm convinced of their mental instability. I've heard them rave, with eyes glazed over, about the heavenly landscapes after a new snow, the crisp, clean air, and what ripping fun it is to careen down a hillside standing on a couple of slippery boards. Well, I can think of better things to do than freeze my behind off while flirting with a compound fracture. For the life of me, I don't know what's wrong with them.

Let's be realistic here. We're looking at the suicide season, complete with lunch hour sunsets. How the heck can one rhapsodize about obstructed walkways, crusty grey globs of remnant snowbanks, and bathtub-sized potholes?

Winter here is profoundly unsexy. The senses become dulled by too little light, itchy alpaca wool, food tainted by snoots full of Vicks VapoRub and lips encased in medicated goo. After 14 years here, I still cannot tell a male from a female with greater than 50% accuracy between November and March. We all lumber around among the other genderless shapes with bitter scowls and parkas the size of cumulus clouds. We women must completely abandon all attempts to reveal our womanly figures. No man worth having is apt to croon, "Wow, look at *that* lump of Gortex-covered down with waterproofed stumps!"

Beneath our down coats, which can also be used as flotation devices or featherbeds, it only gets worse, since most of us are out of shape from months of holiday glee and low-impact hibernation. Add to this that by simply removing your hat, you can cause your hair to stand straight out from your head as if you've been scared out of your wits. This makes others titter and point, which gets on your nerves in no time flat. Deep, bleeding crevices in your lips and nose are common problems. In fact, every unlovely wintry discomfort you can think of is *pro forma*.

Personally, I find it a stiff challenge to remain positive and clear-headed. As a freelancer, it becomes difficult even to plan the day. Here's a typical scenario:

"Mmm. Let's see. First I'll brush my teeth. Or maybe I should have lunch first. Better have a quick breakfast first. Then I'll meditate. Nah, first a nap and then meditate. Then I can spend some time being confused before moping. Wait. The news is on at noon. I can watch that, brood a bit, read my mail and then meditate. I'm exhausted. Need a nap. It must be the antibiotics. Hey, I got it! Today I'll change out of my pajamas! I could muck about in some sort of mohair ensemble with thermal underthings. Perhaps I should comb my hair. Nah, I'll just mess it up during my next nap . . ."

What's really pathetic is that I think all this *aloud,* as I pace around the house shivering, with my dog following me attentively.

Sitting for hours, with either a remote control or my head in my hands, I ponder getting hooked on phonics. I watch another *Perry Mason* rerun in its entirety before griping that it's the same one I watched last week. I wonder if watching *Jeopardy* will be enough to keep my mind keen till spring.

I buy clothes from catalogs just so I can try them on in the privacy and comfort of my own home. It breaks the monotony. If I'm feeling better by the time they arrive, I take it as a sign that I should a) keep them or b) return them. Either way, I feel certain that I've made the right decision for the right reason.

I only hope that my neighbors can't see me making up my own Tai Chi form in costumes I'd never wear out of the house . . . not that I plan to leave the house anytime soon. . . . On the bright side, I've taught my dog to respond to some amusing alternative commands, such as, "Slap leather, fatso," and "Time to cha-cha, Susan." And I've become quite adept at blowing my nose to the tune of "The Yellow Rose of Texas." Sometimes I listen to Puccini while removing my cuticles with an Exacto blade and chanting the word, "Blistex." Sure, it gets weird, but New England winters aren't for everyone. They are certainly not for me, so I must call upon all of my resources to get by. How, you might ask, have such elaborate survival techniques evolved in an otherwise normal life? Well, 1) I'm a veteran of many Boston winters, and 2) I believe in preparing for the worst, because (see 1).

My friends have suggested I get myself a set of those lights that you sit in front of every day in the winter months to cure Seasonal Affective Disorder. In fact, *all* of my friends got together and confronted me with this suggestion in a very strong way. But I say intervention is unnecessary. I'm only reacting the way any sane person would to my environment! It's all those people who take their pajamas off every day and go out into traffic that are the crazy ones. (Have you ever heard of a terrorist, rapist or troublemaker of any type who left his pajamas on and didn't leave home? I rest my case.)

I have my safety gauges: I take comfort in the fact that I can move to another ecosystem anytime I want. My boyfriend keeps a carry-on bag packed with sunblock, bathing suits and passports near the door, just in case things get . . . you know . . . like last winter—extreme.

So listen, if you're thinking of relocating anywhere north of Norfolk, plan on enjoying fireplaces, hot toddies, making soup and renting movies. That'll see you through till January at best. But be forewarned:

Along about March, we'll all be so sickened by the whole winter mess that we'll join in a chorus of "Fuck the savings account, we're goin' to Barbados!" And should you turn out to be one of those cross-country knuckleheads, please, just keep it to yourself.

Thank you for listening.

There have been plenty of times when having a two-person family didn't quite constitute a party—times when I'd try to compensate by drinking a couple of glasses of wine even though I knew it would probably give me a killer migraine. Anything to take the focus off all that was missing.

Telling time
The thirty-ninth turkey.

1988

Billie called and asked me to co-hostess a Thanksgiving dinner for our friends at the mansion where she rents a room.

My daughter was spending this holiday with her grandparents, and, in some ways, I was relieved to be disburdened of the responsibility for a traditional feast attended by just the two of us. Turkey or no turkey, since Cynthia and I see each other every day, there's very little left for us to say to each other that makes for a festive occasion. In fact, the harder we try, the more pitiful our Thanksgivings become. My suggestion last year—to dine by candlelight wearing our best dresses—only heightened the sense of what

121

was missing. By the time we sat down, I was exhausted from cooking and she was grouchy from having to help.

In both our cases, friends had invited us to join their families, but I was determined it was not so much about numbers as it was about family. And I was wrong.

So I was happy to throw myself into Billie's project this year. I arrived early at the big stone house called Graycliff. Billie and I sang as we made pies and placed candles all around. We stoked the fire and decorated the enormous hearth. When everything was in place, we changed into pretty velvet dresses and spritzed ourselves with perfume.

A flurry of kissed cheeks, compliments and covered dishes were punctuated by the doorbell. In they came, lightly dusted with snow, passing their coats to Billie or to me, and populating the kitchen with holiday outcasts. It was as if we had all agreed not to mention where we weren't that day, and to make the best of being together.

We took our seats at the long sparkling table and someone said a toast to our friendship. I clinked glasses with the people near enough to reach: Jim and Sharon Barrett, careening toward divorce since the horrible death of their only daughter, who was hit by a drunk driver two Halloweens ago;

klink. klink.

An old boyfriend of mine who came to dinner alone and gave me a still-wounded look before the first of too many drinks;

klink.

And Billie, who's making the best of yet another year without a boyfriend, much less a baby.

"To us!"

The mood was bittersweet. Not a person there had made it to that table unscathed by one of life's unseemly turns. Two women, seated at opposite ends of the room, suffered each other's company after an old, unresolved argument, the topic of which none of us could even remember. Yet we were together, so we laughed and loved each other up, and made it a wonderful time.

Was this the kind of Thanksgiving adults were having back when I was a carefree kid, sliding down a banister and playing tag with my brothers? I don't remember them sighing like we did, nor can I recall a hard laughter that verged on weeping, like that which rose from our table at Billie's that night.

After dinner and several glasses of wine, I put on an apron and began to clean up. Groups of people gathered here and there to chat and finish their coffee. Then one of the other Graycliff residents brought a troop of her 19-year-old friends in to raid our leftovers. They congregated in the kitchen, ignoring me. I glanced over my shoulder and made eye contact with one of the young girls when a chilling thing occurred: I saw myself through her eyes.

I was an older lady in a velvet dress and apron, with

bright yellow rubber gloves, washing Thanksgiving dishes.

It seemed as though my life had gone by just that fast, as if I had moved from their sneakers to my suede pumps in the time it takes to break a dish.

The worst is behind me now

Coping with a big butt.

1995

I couldn't be more tickled with myself. Just when I thought I could relax and accept at long last my common middle-aged figure, I decided to give vanity one more go. After all, I'm an American woman. Here, it's a cultural given that we will attempt whatever it takes to swim up the stream of our own DNA, spit in the face of forces such as gravity, even become bulimic, or as the great Malcolm X said in reference to something else, achieve our goal "by any means necessary." The goal here is, of course, to look like a 10-year-old boy, if at all possible.

This is a tall order, since women in my family have looked like Rubens models since earliest recorded history. We have soft, cherubic bellies and butts made for long hours of sitting on a milking stool next to a cow. A 16th-century tapestry depicts Huguenot Radant women fleeing France with their meaty keisters wobbling close behind them. Today's Radant females, if left unattended by a personal trainer, default to this same shape, which is no longer all the rage.

Seeing as I had an awful lot of other things to do, I had pretty much decided to forego the enormous effort it takes to go against nature. Silly me, I figured I might just accept looking like a 45-year-old member of my own family. This process is also known as "letting oneself go" in today's argot. It's frowned upon. So call me crazy, but I did an eleventh-hour about-face and set out to give sineminess one last shot.

And here's the part where I'm so darned tickled with myself. You know how people always try to tell you that you get wiser with age and therefore life gets easier? Well, here's a show of wisdom: I decided to write down the few remaining workout regimens I had *not* tried as a younger woman. This boiled down to a short list:

1. Uneven parallel bars. (Too much upper body work.)
2. Figure skating. (Good for getting anthracite glutes, but frankly, I'm not a big fan of sequins.)
3. Greco-Roman wrestling. (Bingo!)

I went to my neighboring town of Cambridge, where one can find literally any form of training known to man. And sure enough, tacked up on a light pole in Harvard Square: *Greco-Roman wrestling, 343 Dunster Street, second floor, weeknights at 6:30 and 9:00. Saturdays at 10:00, noon and 4:00.*

The key to this workout is to get yourself in the correct weight and age class. Don't be nosy about my weight class. All you need to know is that I'm not easily tipped over. I was fortunate to find an introductory level Baby Boomer class for non-smoking single women on Tuesday and Thursday nights. They weren't particular about my height.

The wrestling studio, known as "the arena," was lined with posters of everyone from Hugh Grant to Gore Vidal and (who knew?) Connie Chung, each in a semi-mooning pose, as if they were just bending over to pick up a contact lens when the photographer called their names and forced them to turn around with casual facial expressions. In a gilded frame near the credit card imprint machine was an enlarged photo of my coach, Marlene "Sweety" Lopez, crammed into a La-Z-Boy recliner with two other tight-heinied Greco-Roman wrestlers, grinning ear to ear.

My first bout was with a 46-year-old new grandmother named Doris. She was so enamored of her new family member that her focus was off. She showed me pictures of her little wrinkly grandbaby before our match, and I decided to use the word "Grandma" to get her goat if she fought dirty and I had to resort to trash talking. After our cordial greeting, the viewing of the snapshots and some preliminary instruction, Doris and I locked arms and began pushing and grunting like we were the same dress size at a Bloomingdale's sale. You better believe our buttock muscles got a thorough working. These muscles are the body's brakes, and buddy, when you've got a moose like Doris honked off at you, you'd better pump those brakes.

My hunch that wrestling would prove to be a perfect choice for firming the rear paid off in the end. I had physical proof just 48 hours after I first tangled with Doris, when my glutes were glutted with lactic acid such that I had to call the fire department to help me get out of bed.

Still I persevered, noting that I had never seen a Greco-Roman wrestler with an unwieldy *tuchas*. And after only eight weeks of dedicated wrestling, I was the proud owner of an ass you could crack an egg on. My coach was so proud of my progress that he apparently contacted some fitness video producers and invited them to Thursday night's clash of the middle-aged titans. After a rigorous match, a trim younger man approached me and asked if I would be interested in starring in a prime time TV special about fit Boomers entitled *Hindsight*. Sort of a motivational *Buns of Steel* show for the over-forty set, hosted by Katie Couric. The downside was that I would be paid scale and would not be privy to my interview questions before the taping. Also, the producer's assistant said I'd have to wear a thong for the taping, and that's when I turned him down cold. "I'm no show-off," I said confidently. And that's the beauty of having a toned caboose like mine. Confidence.

Then something really disturbing happened. I woke up. And man, was I hungry.

100 Center Street

Everything's done and it's time to lie down.

1982

I'm trying to ignore the old man with a cane coming my way. He's crumpled and stooped and struggling to complete every step before patiently contemplating his next. It's way too late for him to be out on this balmy night. And I know his presence will tempt muggers and meanies who now roam the neighborhood after dark. I bet he's around 90 years old. Anyway, he's far too old to be *anywhere* at *any* hour unattended. But there he is, this frail remnant of vitality, barely on balance, and all I can think of is what his ancient skull will sound like when it hits the sidewalk.

"Not tonight," I grumble to myself, turning up my Walkman. I've had a rough day in the single-parent business and one of my clients was daring me to take him to court. I deserved those hits of pot I just had and the musical accompaniment on my evening stroll. My need to be aloft with music and freedom has never felt more urgent than on this night.

The old man stumbles, stability eluding him. I *could* just keep going—I don't have to take care of *every* situation personally. He probably lives at 100 Center Street with the other decalcifying, infirm Jewish people who cluster in Brookline group homes. They sit on park benches and bellow to each other about their conditions, answering back with "What?" or "Oy!" They drive enormous American cars way past the time they can see, going no more than 5 m.p.h., making daredevil brake-free turns or, worse, driving a straight mile with a flashing turn signal, pumping the brakes intermittently. They drop like flies only to be fetched by agony wagons that cart them to a nearby hospital and then bring them back to their park bench stations to tell the tale.

The old man is only two blocks from 100 Center Street. I just glanced back to check. But why is this old buzzard out at 11:00 P.M.? It'll be midnight before he makes it home.

He doesn't hear the click of my Walkman shutting down, nor the sigh of thwarted freedom I give as I make my decision. He doesn't see me crossing the street. I'm afraid I'll startle him, so I start speaking as I slowly approach. He doesn't act like a vulnerable old man alone in the night with a likelihood of falling down and an inability to get up. He doesn't have the good sense to be afraid of me. I must look enormous to him, towering a full foot over his downy grey head. I don't think I could carry him, though, if he fell. I'm afraid he'd break. "Mind if I walk with you a spell?" I repeat, remembering that my grandmother used to say things like that. And I extend my arm like an usher seating the wedding guests.

All this strikes me as comical. Of course, I'm stoned . . . but here I am, a strapping, corn-fed Midwestern young mother, fairly under the influence, breaking from responsibility, having just turned off some pissy rock music to escort a tintype relic half my size to wherever he was bound in the middle of the night. He loops his knuckly hand in the crook of my elbow and holds on, gripping his cane in the other. And we walk at a snail's pace, pausing for eight or nine labored breaths before taking another step. "Where you headed, sir?" I say so the entire block can hear me. And he answers in little more than a whisper. "I took the bus. Just got out of the hospital today. And I'm ready to go."

Yeah, but where's he going? And why so late? Where's he been since he was released from the hospital?

I hear myself speaking to him as if he were a child. "Well, you're sure enough out here on the street tonight, and goin', but where?—Say, what's your name? My name is Christine, and I bet I'm your neighbor." We stop on the sidewalk. His once-upon-a-time neck, now consumed by a humpy upper back, moves almost audibly as he turns to look at me. "Mr. Parks. How'd y'do, Chrissy." And for an instant, I

132

look deeply into those red-rimmed eyes at what looks like a century. "My wife died six weeks ago . . . and then I got sick and had to go to the hospital . . . And now I'm ready to go," he tells me between gaping pauses.

Aw, jeez—this old fossil's talking about dying! I give up my mental health walk to offer this guy safe passage home and now he's fixin' to buy the farm! I immediately picture a scene involving illuminated porch lights, a murmuring crowd, medical personnel, a host of investigative reporters, cops taking down my name and wanting to ask me a few questions. Then tomorrow's newspaper story about the stoned woman found alone with the old man's body in the middle of the night. For a moment, I'm oddly steamed at Mr. Parks. Then it gives way to resignation: we're stuck with each other, like it or not, and it'll be a while before we reach the corner.

"You have any relatives around here?" I ask, hoping I can pass the proverbial baton. "No," he huffs. "Who are your friends . . . I mean, do you belong to any social clubs or anything?" "Only my current events group. It was just somethin' to do, but it isn't enough," Mr. Parks says with a shoo-fly gesture. "What's a current events group?" I ask, hoping to burn up some of the silence between here and that distant corner. Between gasps for air, he tells me that each member of the group is assigned a country or region to follow in the news. Then when they have meetings, everyone is obliged to report their findings and a lively discussion is supposed to follow. "For years, I was stuck with the Middle East," he says with pure scorn, "then finally, someone from the group had to go to a nursing home, and he was a fella who covered Canada. I begged them to let me trade for Canada, for cryin' out loud."

And just as I ask if they let him, a car the size of a barge drives by. "That looks like my car," Mr. Parks said. A fleeting thought about inheriting the old man's parking space makes me feel ashamed of myself. But one of my many burdens these days is the place I park my car a half mile from my apartment.

"You park your car—I mean, you live at 100 Center Street, don't you, Mr. Parks?" And he grumbles something that sounds affirmative. ("Well I hope so, because I don't have the *patience* to take you any further at this pace," I mutter to myself.) "I'm sorry you lost your wife. I imagine it's devastating to lose a spouse," I say like a flip young know-it-all, "but y'know, people rally and life can offer plenty more if you just . . . hang on. Anyway, who's going to report on Canada . . . if . . .?" I don't know what I'm talking about and he knows it, shooting me a glance that says, "Hush up, young'n." This is getting worse.

"Nope. I've done everything. I'm tired now, and I want to go." End of discussion.

"So this is your place, eh?" I attempt to confirm as we enter the lobby at 100 Center Street. He thanks me for my kindness, heads to the elevator and says goodnight. His eyes find me once more. I'm probably the last person he'll ever see. A complete stranger who can't relate to his honorable place in the last hours of his life. I don't believe he's strong enough to remain standing when the elevator stops on his floor. "Shall I see you up to your apartment?" I say, thinking he ought not to be letting strangers up to his door in the middle of the night. "Very well," he says, standing under a flickering fluorescent light, and we take the stale-smelling elevator to Mr. Parks' floor, where we simply say goodnight. His door latches before my voice whines, "You take care . . ."

At the phone booth on the corner, Directory Assistance gives me the phone number at 100 Center Street. The woman on duty thanks me for seeing Mr. Parks home, and assures me that she'll see to it that he gets meals sent up; she doesn't think I'll have to pay for them, but takes my number and thanks me for offering.

I return to my apartment on Winchester, look in on my sleeping teenaged daughter, and stand in front of a mirror for a while, changed.

Her Royal Highness
An unforgettable Christmas in London.

1983

I daresay it was a Christmas like none other. Rather than coming at the speed of twinkling lights, the big day seemed as though it would never arrive. Perhaps that was due to a lack of frantic shopping and an absent deadline for wrapping and delivery. We had decided not to buy gifts that year, so while everyone else sped through malls wild-eyed and panting, I, my then-boyfriend Seth, and my teenaged kid drummed our fingers on the table, mustering patience. It was 1983 and Seth, one of the Chosen People, had announced his deep and abiding lack of enthusiasm for this Christian-based, retail-priced holiday. I, being a single parent, had always been obliged to be Santa-like and festive, which presented an annual problem, given my income and temperament. But 1983 was a year in which things just seemed to drop into place. My daughter Cynthia, a surly 15-year-old, was no longer charmed by my meager attempts at Christmas cheer. She showed open contempt for my Hawaiian Christmas album, especially when I hula-ed and sang along. My presents were barely ever more than adequate. Basically, she loathed me and was abjectly horrified by my proximity to her. I kept myself busy not taking any of this personally. So the three of us decided to plan a memorable-but-giftless Christmas by purchasing tickets to London.

A few weeks before our departure, I looked up my one and only British pal, Rebecca, for some tips on what to see and where to go. Becca was a mysterious mix of proper Brit and little scamp. I knew her from the vegetarian restaurant on Newbury Street where I had often lunched. Over the many years she had waited tables and I had dined there, I'd slowly gotten to know her. In the beginning, Becca's behavior was extremely formal and by-the-book. She complimented me regularly on my "frocks," saying they were "lovely, indeed." Then over time, I learned that the hickey on her neck was from a violin and the twinkle in her eye from a charming brand of wickedness. She was and still is an accomplished classical violinist and violist. But it was the wickedness I was attracted to. One fine day, when she delivered an order of brown rice and vegetables to my table, I found a plastic cockroach on the plate, and I knew without a doubt that we would become good friends. Sure enough, in years to come, I would introduce Becca to marijuana, Aretha Franklin and skinny-dipping. But that's another story.

We met for tea and discussed my upcoming trip to her homeland. Rebecca made recommendations suitable to each of the members of our party. For my heavily eye-lined daughter, we'd visit the punk shops on the Old King's Road in Chelsea. For me, she guessed Portobello Road and Petticoat Lane flea markets. And for Seth, we'd visit Golders Green, the Jewish section, where he could eat Chosen food, and we could all go visit Becca's Christian parents, who lived there. It was a kind invitation, to which I clung, for fear of losing all contact with my longstanding tradition of Christmas melancholia. For me, this would be the high point of the vacation, spending Boxing Day (the day after Christmas) with *someone else's* family; no gifts, lots of food. There'd be a Christmas tree there and all that familiar good will. Perhaps it would even have an Olde English feel to it! Yes, Boxing Day with the Wiggins family would be emotional spackling for the absence of my Christmas.

In exchange for all this hospitality, I offered to cart Becca's gifts to her family. This made me feel oddly weepy, knowing that among them there would be nothing for us to open. Never mind that *having* gifts to open on Christmases past had also left me weepy. Becca handed me the phone number and address of her parents along with directions from Heathrow to Chelsea, via the tube.

Our bed-and-breakfast in Chelsea was a bit chilly,

but we were thrilled to be there. There were a few things missing among the accommodations, like face cloths and actual coffee, but hey! We slept off our jet lag and awoke with sniffles and sore throats. Without real coffee to jolt us back into consciousness, we felt fortunate to have in its stead the bracing effects of the cold rain.

Out and about in London, Cynthia, my lovely overstated teen, was indistinguishable from all the other black-clad, spiky-haired, angry young punks of the mid-eighties. And that's exactly how she liked it. If I took my eye off her for a moment, Miss Blendo would disappear into the mob of snarling trendoids and it would be up to me to find her. There were times when I considered letting her panic about where Seth and I were so that it wasn't entirely my job to keep us together. But I realized that at age 15, she dreamt of just such an opportune moment when, due to my neglect, she could embark on an exciting life on the street, among her people. London would likely suit her even better than Brookline, Massachusetts. So I tromped around London in the freezing drizzle, with a coffee-withdrawal headache, watching my daughter like a hawk, and listening to the occasional "Oy!" of my boyfriend when things got too Christmasy.

I rang up Becca's family (you know, that's how they talk over there. They say things like "ring you up," and even worse). Her brothers, both classical musicians as well, were there, and Steven, the French horn player, made the arrangements with me for Boxing Day. He was astonishingly enthusiastic about our meeting, or maybe that was politeness. Anyway, he was "ever so chipper" and kept saying things like, "righty-o, then." I couldn't believe it. I figured these British people must really pour it on for us foreigners. No way they really spoke like that all the time. Then suddenly, I became apprehensive about Boxing Day, fearing that I couldn't speak English well enough to hang out all day with actual English people who had the language down.

On Christmas Day, we milled around and found a restaurant that could squeeze us in for dinner. I'll be perfectly honest with you, it was weird. Of course, those were the days before I took Prozac, and frankly, most of life stank of imperfection and loss back then. But in our own little ways, each of us pulled through. Seth was oblivious to the whole Christmas thing, so he didn't tune in to my urge to sob on my coq au vin. Cynthia's consistent disapproval of everything was no surprise. The food, of course, sucked, as all English food tends to, and Seth complained that it was overpriced and the portions were small. (If Seth's going to eat food that sucks, he wants lots of it and for a good price.) I just sang "Melekali kimaka," my favorite Hawaiian Christmas carol, under my breath and fought back tears. We trudged home in the penetrating dampness and bedded down for a long night of more penetrating dampness before what promised to be a rainy Boxing Day.

Relieved as I was that our big day had arrived, I must say I was stricken with a bizarre case of shyness as we approached the house where Becca's parents lived in Golders Green. I kept thinking that my daughter would likely not speak a word to anyone and that her hatred of me would be misconstrued as poor manners. Seth, who forever joked around, would undoubtedly say abstractly funny things that wouldn't translate to our hosts, and I was preoccupied that I would, before the day was done, find some reason to blurt out the word "fuck."

Becca's father, Ian Wiggins, was exactly the sort of character a cartoonist would draw of an elderly British subject. His bald head, shaped somewhat like a torpedo, was fringed with a wiry strip of long, white hair. His eyebrows, like cotton balls, were uncombed and hung partially over piercing blue eyes. His fingers were like great links of sausage attached to massive hands, way out of proportion with the rest of him. And of course, there was a fair amount of tweed involved. He taught piano, wrote poetry and painted. He was also a bibliophile, judging from the impressive overloaded bookshelves that lined their living room walls. Ian spoke with a very BBC/Public School sort of accent. He talked without ever really letting his teeth or lips meet entirely, as though his teeth were unattached at the gum and that, by speaking in a muffled fashion, he could keep them all in his mouth. He intermittently made sucking sounds, as though he'd just been clever. I found it difficult to grok what he said most of the time. Yet his eyes shone and twinkled, supporting my hunch that he'd just said something ribald, so I chuckled a lot and nodded yes when spoken to.

Monique, Becca's mum, was 15 or 20 years younger and French, which may have accounted for Ian's twinkling eyes; who knows? Very pretty and petite, Monique flew about the house hostessing and insisting we not pay any mind to the fact that she had a splitting migraine (pronounced meeeegrain). She spoke very quickly, with a Franco-British accent and generally with both hands over her eyes, so I couldn't make out what she said either. But I knew she felt awful, so when Monique addressed me, I responded with a sympathetic moan and patted her forearm. Meanwhile, my daughter kept catching my eye, making faces that meant, "Let's get out of here!" All this happened in the first five minutes.

We were also trotted around to meet a dozen other Boxing Day celebrants, all of whom seemed to be professors, historians or philosophers. I could not remember any of their names, so I just referred to everyone as Nigel or Angus as I coughed into a napkin to cover my mistake. Thank heaven, Monique was an excellent vegetarian cook. "Well, now *that's* something!" I thought to myself, stacking my plate high with food and finding a cozy chair.

Soon everyone had settled into a seat, creating a large conversation pit that remained uncomfortably devoid of conversation for what seemed like a decade. I looked around the circle and found that the only people smiling painfully through blank stares were the Americans. My extremities grew numb and I was unable to inhale deeply.

Finally, Monique cracked the ice (a bag of which she held to her head, by the way) and asked what we had been doing since we'd arrived in London.

"Well, for a few days, we asked Londoners what the Queen's last name is, as we made our way around the city," I piped up. But my voice sounded alien and way too loud, as if I had spoken through a blow horn. "Um, it was pretty funny, really, because no one seemed to know for certain. Heh. Heh. Heh-heh." I sounded like an idiot. And also like I was making fun of Brits for being ignorant.

"Well, they all had reasonable guesses," I said, digging myself in further, "such as Hapsburg, Tudor, Regina, and of course, Windsor." The room was so still, you could hear Ian's eyebrows furrowing like the sound of Velcro ripping in an adjoining room. "But-but, hey, I'd be easily fooled, you know, because what do I know about British royalty? Not much, I'll tell you that. I mean, I *think* Queen Victoria ruled for a long spell, but that's about as far as I go on your, um . . . monarchy."

I could feel my eyes darting back and forth as though I were watching some imaginary Ping-Pong match. I felt as though I might vomit my baba ganouj. Then Ian took pity on me, leapt up from his chair and removed a large, dusty book from one of his shelves and flipped through the pages. "Yes," he said, taking charge, "It says here that Victoria was on the throne for *64 years!*" And then he looked back at me. Again, time stood still, and the room full of English strangers all stared at me, leaning forward just a tad in anticipation. I could hear my heart thumping. I didn't know what to say to that.

"Whoa, she must've had a hell of a ring around her fanny!" I said, astonishing myself. And with that, every single person in the room straightened their spines with a snapping motion, bolting up erect in their chairs as though they'd been startled by a cannon blast. And no one made eye contact with me. Through my sudden-onset tinnitus, I could hear people clearing their throats and shifting nervously in their chairs. I knew I had gone too far, but couldn't imagine that a mere toilet joke would render such a reaction—even in Britain, so I leaned toward a young woman to my right and whispered, "What does 'fanny' mean here in England?" The acoustics in that living room were darn good. Everyone could clearly hear my query. She blinked spastically about 300 times, raised her hand over her mouth and stuttered, "It's the . . . female . . . genitalia!"

I had said the British equivalent of the word "pussy" in front of my *girlfriend's family* on *Boxing Day*. And I had said it in reference to *their Queen!* I assure you, I would never *ever* use that word in any language, even in reference to a kitty cat! I felt my fingers darting in and out of my hairline as my body folded over forward and my elbows hit my knees. A loud, low whirring sound made me feel as though I were tripping. Seth and Cynthia both stared at me, eyebrows raised and mouths agape. And that damned

Hawaiian Christmas song started going through my head again.

The next thing I remember was Seth stuffing my elbow into my coat for me and leading Cynthia and me towards the tube station.

I'm told that the aftermath of my *faux pas* wasn't so horrible, and that word later circulated that the word "fanny" in American is not the least bit vulgar. Some people even found it somewhat endearing in retrospect, but I don't remember anything after insulting Her Majesty. My amnesia lasted, luckily, through our return trip to the States.

The following Christmas, Seth and I went to a Jewish deli in Brookline. Cynthia visited her paternal grandparents. It snowed that year, so I got all carried away with holiday spirit and wore a green coat and a red beret to the deli. I was the Goyische Poster Girl, with rosy cheeks and blond curls springing from under my hat. Everybody looked at me as if I were lost when I walked in. I remember at least one bored-stiff chosen person per booth, leaning on a fist so one cheek was all scrunched up under one eye.

Man, did I ever miss being with my parents in Pittsburgh and listening to Dad play the Wurlitzer.

Someday I'm going to be one righteous grandmother. But right now, as I explained to my daughter, I just don't have the right outfits.

We're next

A Baby Boomer's report on sunny Florida.

1995

The doorbell rang at 5 P.M. today, and there stood Larry, the neighborhood mailman, with a smirk on his face and my checkbook in his hand. "You mailed your checkbook, Chris. Another carrier gave it to me since you're on my route." Cringing, I thanked him and hurried to shut the door. "Must be due to travel fatigue," I said to myself, and rushed back up the stairs.

The trip from which I was still recovering was a visit to the North American burial grounds in Florida where my parents, along with everyone else's parents, are retired to. It was an unusual visit, marked by an increased tolerance for the company of the older generation. The tiring aspect of this trip was not the travel itself, but a driving urge to figure out why *this time was so different. And my conclusion was very unsettling, indeed:*

While in Florida I saw, plain as day, the signs of transition—from being a driven, type-A, hip and smug Baby-Boomer-with-an-attitude, to a dozing, People *magazine-reading snackmeister who might at any moment begin to dabble in watercolors. Next stop in this transition: three-wheeled bicycles, leathery tans, and those Monday-Tuesday-Wednesday medication boxes. Think about it, Buck-O.* We're next.

When my plane touched down in Ft. Lauderdale, I leapt out of my seat, grabbed my PowerBook and carry-on bag, and bolted toward the aircraft's port. Uttering something vaguely polite to the b-byeing airline personnel, I rushed past the masses of dawdling elderly, through the terminal and down to the baggage claim area to meet my folks. As I stood on the curb, trying to spot my silver-haired parents, who now look surprisingly like everyone else's, I took a few deep breaths of warm Florida air. And the weirdest thing happened.

I relaxed.

My usual restlessness with Mom and Pop's pace didn't get its grip on me. By golly, I enjoyed letting the folks prattle on and on about nothing in particular. This was a huge improvement over my old habit of sighing loudly and reminding them that I had no idea who or what they were talking about. I think they enjoyed my transformation too. And for the rest of that first day, time seemed to saunter past me gently, dripping with humidity and calm. This was the opposite of my usual relationship with time, which is to rip through each day like a maniac hacking her way through a jungle. The pleasure was so exotic it was as though I were on some sort of mind-altering drug. My tolerance for television increased measurably each day I stayed. My PowerBook served as a fascinating conversation piece with Mom and Dad, but I couldn't bring myself to work much. Instead, I read, napped and snacked. Pooh-poohing the notion of fitness, I enjoyed brief, sweat-free walks around their small retirement community and noticed feeling energized afterwards rather than completely wiped. I felt so good, I even decided I'd go with Mom and her girlfriend on Thursday night to play my very first game of Bingo.

Mom's friend, Gabby, who's a bit younger than Mom and maybe 10 years my senior, came by early for impromptu coffee and a leisurely chat. I tried to imagine such a luxury in my life back in Boston, but could not. Gabby formed a bridge between Mom and me, so there was no palpable generation gap. Actually, the three of us were having a pretty nice time and decided to take advantage of an Early Bird Special (whatever that was) before Bingo. I was game to go along on any event with the word "special" in it.

Over trays of lasagna and chicken breasts, we discussed which hair colors adequately cover the gray. Each of us presented billfold photos of our grown-up children to each other, reciting their names in that love-struck tone. Smiling, and mentally singing, "You've got a friend," I looked at my mom and her buddy with a bit of envy for their simpler, quieter lives. I knew that after I returned to Boston to slay dragons again, they'd still be sitting on the screened-in porch, waving to the neighbors, giggling and snapping playing cards down on the kitchen table after dinner. I felt a strange homesickness for this place I'd never been to—yet. For the first time, I wasn't a total outsider to the mobile home world my mom and dad inhabited. I puffed up a little at the thought that this might be a product of my hard-won and tardy maturity. Then I remembered with a start, and whispered as I stared glassy-eyed into my creamed corn, "Oh God, I'm next."

Mailing my checkbook made me take stock of my quirks. You know—the ones that transform into eccentricities, which, with enough mileage, can cross the border into out-and-out geriatric loopiness? Sure enough, my collection of paper and plastic bags in the pantry is getting out of control. Also, I discovered that I have a tub of Dippity-Doo in my medicine chest from 1967. I decided I'd better make a list: Indeed, I still refer to my 27-year-old daughter as my kid. Ever since I got my new line-less bifocals, I have to hold onto the rail when descending the stairs. I've run out of storage space. I forget if I've already taken my Prozac. I refer to medications as "my medications." The truth is, I never want to move again. I admit I sometimes fantasize about grandchildren. I will readily decline to do any heavy lifting, citing my bad neck as the problem. Uncomfortable shoes are now out of the question—I don't care *how* beautiful they are. And people in their 20's annoy and amuse me with their self-conscious struggle to demonstrate hipness. I *remember* all that silliness. Okay, okay . . . it's starting.

Is it warm in here or is it just me?

After that first night of Bingo with Mom and Gabby, we were walking home from the Rec Hall, chatting about the merits of small-time gambling, when I suddenly imagined that same luxury trailer park 20 years from now.

The place will be peppered with wrinkly old hippies (my generation) wearing garish, tie-dyed beachwear and shadow dancing to Hendrix cassettes at seniors' events. Most of us will have police records from having been busted for grass. The younger retirees in our group will claim they still do a bitchin' hip-hop. We'll speak in a devout urban slang, saying things like, "Righteous shuffleboard game, girlfriend." And the grandkids will make fun of us for wearing our hats backwards. The folks a decade older, the people whose pictures will be shown on the *Today Show* by a Willard Scott protégé, are the last of a dying breed called Beatniks. Journalists will flock to them with tape recorders and videocams, lighting their cigarettes against doctors' orders just to hear them say things like, "Put me in the clouds, Daddy-O." There'll be damn few of them left 20 years from now, what with all that caffeine, nicotine and bongo-ing. Their old-fashioned ways will be a source of endless fascination to historians and smokers' rights groups.

There's little doubt that some of my girlfriends will still be doing aerobics 20 years from now, perhaps hoisting boxes of dried macaroni in lieu of free weights for their strength training. I can imagine the terrycloth sweatbands upon their crepey brows; the Grateful Dead running suits and "Free Mandela" T-shirts. Our men will camp out beneath their own bellies in hi-tech recliners, staring at televised gymnastic competitions, insisting they "could do that," then belching. We'll know by then to simply give 'em a thumbs-up and offer them another pot brownie. It's good for the glaucoma.

The old 12-step program veterans will affix bumper stickers that read, "Ten minutes at a time" to their huge, unwieldy American automobiles. Karaoke will be very big among the old folks who've not quite abandoned hope of becoming rock stars. This will embarrass our descendants to the core.

I already notice, in fact, a strange, somewhat morbid curiosity about those catalogs full of bric-a-brac shelves, anti-snoring pillows, and men's bedroom slippers shaped like beer cans that make belching sounds when walked in. I admit I already look at every single page and even consider buying some of the strangest items.

I know it's hard to believe, brothers and sisters, but it'll happen. The die is already cast. We'll sit for hours trying, in a nasal drone, to remember the names of things and people and places that make no difference whatever to the long, boring stories we'll tell. All our friends will drop dead one right after another and Keith Richards will outlive us all. We'll have nail fungus ointments in our medicine chests and burping plastic containers in the kitchen cabinets. We'll shamelessly display the photos of our families on every horizontal surface of the living room, as well as to every living being who won't get up and leave the room. It's true, I tell you. I've seen the evidence.

Can you imagine what our grandchildren will think of us?

"Grams, show me your tattoo again? What was that big muddy party you went to where everybody was naked?—Woodstick? Who's that guy Grandpa calls God—you know, that old bald guy you two go listen to down at the Holiday Inn?" "Eric Clapton, honey. And yes, he *is* God."

"Poppy, *why* won't Grandma tell me what 'Steely Dan' means?—She listens to him all the time!?" "Never mind with the Steely Dan again, Dude—go ask Grandma if you can count the holes in her ears. She loves that . . . and then maybe she'll give you one of her special brownies before your nap."

They'll plead with us not to dip down on one arthritic knee and pump our elbows, hissing the word, "Yessss!" when we win at canasta. They'll beg us to turn our music down.

We'll reminisce ad nauseum about the good old

days, back before the turn of the millennium. Colgate will market pesto-flavored denture adhesive just for us. And we'll keep our decaying backstage passes affixed to the fridge by JFK commemorative magnets.

The whole affair promises to be highly embarrassing. But I've just been witness to the fact that when we arrive there, we'll no longer give a damn what other people think.

Frankly, I can't wait.

This is where Stuart Kleinman, President of Egg Pictures, decided I actually was Claudia Larsen (Rick Richter's character) from the movie.

My job on the production crew of *Home for the Holidays*

Thirty-six hours that darn near finished me off.

1995

After a year or so of dropping hints, several months of strategically aiming them, and finally, some shameless groveling, I secured a job on the production crew of *Home for the Holidays*. Despite many warm invitations to just come and watch the filming in comfort, I pushed for the crew job and got it.

My mission was to make myself useful while on the set of this movie, which was a byproduct of my own short story. I had somewhat romantic ideas about being a part of this other family, comprised of the production crew and cast. I preferred this vision to that of me standing around on the sidelines, not knowing what to do with my hands, and blushing.

Originally, the exteriors were to be shot in Massachusetts near my home, but since it was impossible to start the filming until February, the venue had to be changed to a city farther south, Baltimore, in order to make it look Novemberish. For some reason, this wasn't enough to dissuade me, so through a friend of a friend, who long ago lived in Baltimore, I found a lead on a home there for my month-long production gig.

Peggy Rajske, the film's producer, thoughtfully put me in a position smack dab in the heart of the action, where I could watch everything being filmed. I was to be a set p.a. (production assistant), a position at the very bottom of the film production food chain. And no amount of warning could talk me out of it.

Finding a Baltimore home-away-from-home finally materialized just two and a half weeks before my job was to begin. It was right around the same time that my 10-year-old Subaru quit on me. Harry, my lovable Greek mechanic, called with the bulletin: "I gotta bad noose." There was very low compression ("compresh") on the left side of my Subaru's engine and it would cost $400 to $500 for Harry to take the car apart just to see if it was salvageable. So, for several days, I had a p.a. job in Baltimore, no clue about what that meant, no place to live and no car in which to get there.

Have I mentioned I love adventure?

After a minor freak-out, I got through to Barb and her 19-year-old son, Ethan, in Baltimore. They seemed very nice and said I could stay in their spare bedroom. I promised them they wouldn't see much of me once the gig began, due to the long hours.

As for transportation, I found shopping for a decent used car a time-consuming and unpleasant task. Other people's cars smelled funny. Plus I had the sneaking suspicion that the owners were lying to me.

Finally, in an anxious moment, I bought a new-smelling Ford Escort (I held out for one with heat) and packed it with only the bare necessities: Bright yellow rubber pants, goose-down feather bed, boom box and cassette tapes, lumberjack plaid wool shirt, reflective ankle bands, three kinds of perfume, flashlight, silk and wool undies, camera, picnic basket, over-the-knee socks, sunblock, chemical toe heaters to put in my shoes, laptop computer, floss, tweezers, itty-bitty book light, some flares, two down pillows, framed pictures of my boyfriend and daughter, a hair dryer, cold and flu medications, my Eddie Bauer down jacket, makeup, floppy disks, an assortment of earrings, a pair of ski pants, a push-up bra, Prozac, a bungee cord, medicated lip balm, three maps of Baltimore, spring water and some Tums.

When my departure date arrived, I squeezed into my bulging Ford and, with my head barely poking out of the cargo, I realized I looked like Claudia in the first act of the movie, after she gets fired. I drove six hours to Mount Holly, N.J., and stayed in a HoJo. The next day, some sort of snafu prevented me from being able to move into the house in Baltimore for one more day. So I drove an hour past Baltimore to Reston, VA, where I stayed with friends. The following morning, they fed me French toast and packed me off for the hour's drive back to Baltimore.

There my host family, Barb and Ethan, greeted me with hugs, helped me unload the Ford, and invited me into Ethan's room (sort of a reggae 'chill' grotto), for a "welcome bong hit." Barb's a little giddy and hyper-active, with a big, warm heart. Ethan is an adorable kid who stays stoned and listens to reggae and has only three responses for every occasion: "Cool," "That'll work," and "No problem."

Sleep like there's no tomorrow.

My next task was to impose a restful sleep over the excitement, jittery fatigue and disorientation. I tried to be ready for anything. I knew that being a p.a. was anything but glamorous. Still, I imagined myself becoming the darling of the crew, cracking dry little jokes and being a solid comrade in the weird battle of moviemaking.

I got up at 3:00 A.M. to make a 4:48 call downtown. Due to a bad case of busy legs and head noise, I had only had two hours of sleeping like there was no tomorrow when my new travel alarm started to beep. Since the first day of shooting was at Baltimore–Washington International Airport, my initial job was to load crew members into airport-bound vans and count heads. I was instructed to make the vans leave on time in order to to teach a lesson to dawdlers."

For these reasons, I believe I made a rather unlovely first impression upon the crew, chasing the set designer and sound men around, demanding names so I could check them off my list. In addition to sending off the vans every fifteen minutes, I was to receive and forward incoming pager messages, and then hightail it to the airport to herd extras around the airport set.

Once at Baltimore–Washington International, I was also in charge of redirecting pedestrian traffic, delivering boxes of mail to crew members, phoning the production office with camera times, taking lunch orders for the stars, and of course, snagging the walkie-talkie crossfire that pertained to me. Oh, and also taking orders from everyone who knew I was a rookie. To say I was overwhelmed doesn't even come close. In fact, words fail me entirely.

I would compare it to volunteering at a hospital and being sent into the emergency room with handfuls of unmarked medications to treat dying patients . . . on live network TV. Oh, and all the patients were dressed just like the doctors, some of whom were sleeping on gurneys. And my real job is at Roto Rooter in Trenton. Kinda like that.

Despite my month-long preparation, a few lies told to Radio Shack employees ("Yeah, I' been thinkin' about buying some walkie-talkies . . . can I handle some of yours?"), and a regimen of stamina-building ginseng and sublingual B-12, I was utterly unprepared for the job.

Part of it was my advanced age. For good reason, I was the only 45-year-old p.a. there—and probably in the history of cinema. Part of it was the difficult location for the first two days. Part of it was that I couldn't tell the fake passengers from the real passengers from the crew members. I was yelled at by loved ones coming to greet passengers, and by tightly wrapped fear-of-flying patients who were not yet sedated for their trips. Another big problem was that I'm not clairvoyant.

Communication among the crew could've been better, but *everybody* was in over their heads, and we just had to get our shots and get the hell out of the way, before the airport powers booted us out and ruined everything. But some essential things were overlooked. For example, I understood that I would be given a pager and a cel phone and shown how to work them. This didn't happen. The pager was slipped into my hand on the set without a word of instruction. I didn't even know it didn't beep until I later began vibrating. By then, I was so disoriented that I took it to be a symptom of stress or a spiritual epiphany of some sort. Though a production manager at the office recited rather intricate instructions over the pay phone (my cel phone was broken), I was barely able to follow her with people yelling in my headset and the flight announcements booming out and my beltline vibrating.

The broken cel phone was something no one on the set wanted to help me with, so I attempted to push through that problem by placing credit card calls at the pay phones, where I often had to stand in line while people screamed at me on my headset. Finally, I was given an 800 number for the office, which helped some.

We were all instructed to be in constant contact with Bob Wagner, the 2nd a.d. (assistant director). I wish now that I had known to ask what I was supposed to do when he was completely unavailable for stupid questions like, "Hey Bob—when you say, 'Put Buzz on a van and send him to base camp,' *Who's* Buzz, *where* are the vans and *where/what* is base camp?" Similar jargon problems occurred when I was told to help craft services break down and move. Was I looking for a cart where a guy dispensed Scotch tape and scissors? Where was he moving to? Would *he* know? Turned out that craft services is the concession stand for the cast and crew. Whoever came up with the name craft services for this was in the wrong business.

Nothing was ever clear to me. When I *did* find someone with whom I could clarify these mysteries, they were noticeably grumpy about answering. I can't say I blame them.

Then there was the time I heard Bob Wagner on the walkie-talkie, pleading for someone at Base Camp to "come in." I was there, and responded. He ordered me to *"tell everyone at Base Camp there is a 20-minute warning."* Right. So I took a deep breath and went around Base Camp, telling *everybody* (truckers, airport maintenance people, pedestrians and so on) that there was a 20-minute warning. They all had a good laugh. Later I discovered that a 20-minute warning was for the stars to head for the set.)

One of my fellow p.a.'s had told me to bring a duffel bag with indoor clothes in it. She said there'd be a room where we'd all keep our gear. But when I brought my duffel bag, script, shooting schedule, etc. to the set and asked Bob where to put it, he (bit his tongue and then) said he didn't know. The upshot of this was that I could barely keep track of where my own stuff was, and was eventually separated from it at a time when I needed to change out of my lovely and flattering foul weather gear.

Around 1:30 in the afternoon, which felt like my bedtime, I was handed a scribbled menu for the stars and told to take their lunch orders. But they were either working or had disappeared immediately after we broke for lunch. (They tend not to stick around and let the onlookers bug them for autographs.) I had no clue about where to find them, or for that matter, where to find my own lunch.

When I finally found catering, I had only enough time for three green beans and some lemonade. Then they told us to go to the next set, wherever that was.

Unidentified people shoved boxes of "important mail" in my hands, saying the stars may have the most urgent messages. But when I attempted to deliver to the few people whose names I knew, I was told it was bad timing. In fact, no one seemed accessible for mail, the bulk of which I put in a safe place. The safe place then moved as I went off on other missions. The boxes went away too. About this, there was no one to ask. I had just fucked up. Everybody seemed to be my superior when they were assigning jobs to me, but never to answer questions I had. Nobody. I always had six missions going and no way to prioritize them. I felt like curling up in a ball and sucking my thumb.

At one point, I turned around and found myself staring at Jodie Foster, who said, "Hey—you're Chris? I was wondering which one you were! It's great to meet you!" But someone was screaming in my headset that they needed me somewhere, and so I have no idea what, if anything, I said to Jodie, or to Holly Hunter, to whom she introduced me. The next thing I knew, I was rushing around, trying to find something. Another first impression gone swimmingly.

Later, I turned to find Rick Richter, the screenwriter, and his wife Susan there, unexpectedly. I threw my arms around the pair of them, putting them in a death grip that must've seemed quite strange. It was at that moment that the still photographer took pictures of me with the Richters, we being the so-called "parents of the project." Unfortunately, I was not clad becomingly, appeared to be smuggling coffee grounds in my lower eyelids, and had a look of terror on my face. I'm sure the photos will show up eventually and might even be used against me.

I did not know there were liquids available for the crew. Though I did, eventually, figure out what "craft services" had on their table, I assumed it to be snacks and liquids set up for the actors and extras . . . not for me. I was seriously bewildered and dehydrated.

Toward the end of that first day, around 10:30 P.M., I was asked to stay behind while the grips cleared out, during which time the room where the battery chargers were kept was locked up for the night. So I faced my second day with a puny battery driving my only means of communication and no one who could help.

My car spun out on the icy highway on the way back to Baltimore, and I got lost in the inner city bad neighborhoods, where I was hassled by four large, scary guys at a stoplight (my blond hair and Massachusetts plate glowing in the dark). By the time I got back to Barb and Ethan's house, I was sobbing. And I couldn't go to sleep.

A few hours later, I had to go back to work. Loading crew out from the hotel went a little more smoothly. I think they collectively decided to avoid dealing with me at all costs, and simply got their heinies onto the van, pronto.

So off to BWI I went, with my weak-batteried walkie-talkie on, when I heard a discussion from the set about Ms. Hunter's request for plain, non-fat yogurt, no fruit. It seemed my fellow production assistants were canvassing the airport for such yogurt to no avail. One person had found non-fat yogurt with strawberries and there was a big buzz about whether or not that would do. So I piped in that I was just pulling into the airport parking lot and would gladly go to a nearby hotel in search of Ms. Hunter's yogurt. I got a go-ahead and turned to follow exit signs out of the garage. I then heard someone call to me on the walkie and ask me to change channels to discuss something. Just as I glanced down to change channels on my walkie, I got a violent, vibrating page from my beltline. Boom—before I knew what happened, I had hit an intersecting car in the airport garage.

That's when the cacophony stopped for a moment and I heard myself say, "No es bueno."

I was willing to suffer through an uncomfortable learning curve, ready to work like the devil, without sleep, and for very little money, but now I had become dangerous.

I realized then that there were several dozen younger, more adept people in line for my job who desperately wanted a future in production, and the best thing I could do was to let that better match happen.

I wept uncontrollably as I packed my walkie-talkie, my vibrating pager, some messages to crew members and an apologetic letter of resignation into a plastic bag, and hailed a van driver. "Take this to my superior back at the terminal," I pleaded with bloodshot eyes the size of fried eggs. And with that, I ended my career in production.

On the drive back to Barb and Ethan's, I realized that I must also leave Baltimore, since I had promised my hosts I'd be quite scarce in their house.

The next day, I loaded my Ford again and drove 10

hours back to Boston, where I had cancelled all other work for the rest of the month.

For two whole weeks after returning home, I drank Pedialyte, a remedy for dehydration. Both my big toenails turned black and threatened to come off altogether. I was a whole pant size smaller.

I have since recovered from all of the above and have ceased waking up in the middle of the night, shouting, "What's my twenty?" (Walkie-talkie talk for "location.")

Retirement from the rigors of production agrees with me, and I am content to get only one credit on the movie.*

---

*The names that are rolling while you put on your coat and leave the theatre belong to some of the hardest-working people you can imagine. Think of my story the next time you watch movie credits roll. Those people stayed and finished. Most are still alive today.

To this day, my parents hold hands when they walk together, and smooch at the drop of a hat. They really are partners in the most tender way. I tried to cultivate that vibe with at least 700 boyfriends before giving up. Then I met Dio, who's a natural.

True love

A survivor of romantic love sets the record straight.

1993

For decades, I chased after a perfect relationship. I thought I knew just what it would look like. (I'd seen all the movies.) Dashing, tall and handsome prince of Latin ancestry sees my inner beauty and can think of nothing else but our wedding day. Our courtship would take place on foreign shores, where I'd wear expensive hats and we'd sip cognac. He would call me "Darling" and protect me with his life. I was a classic tragic romantic with all the emotional scars to prove it.

Then something happened and I could no longer endure the storm that followed my romantic expectations. I didn't want to, in fact, didn't think I could, but I *had* to give up. After a protracted struggle, I resigned myself to future retirement at a beach house with my spinster girlfriends, where we would reminisce, grow crankier and more eccentric, and sew elbow patches on our sweaters. (You've seen the movies.)

* * *

Then *he* came to me. It turns out that life with my true love looks a lot different from any movie, celluloid or imaginary: This morning was typical. I woke up sleep-deprived after a night with my prince. He'd had another one of his nights. For eight straight hours, he clanked and ground his teeth like a wild animal, muttered sleepily, "It isn't fair! *I* have the right-of-way," and "Give me back those chestnuts, stupid!" He honked his nose incessantly and performed mid-air spins, mummifying himself in the covers. And, of course, he snored. I looked over at him this morning, bursting with love and a trace of loathing. He turned to me and proffered a spiky kiss on my cheek. His hair shaped like Gumby, his morning smile like the Son of Sam's. Ruby, our 5-lb. terrier puppy, who sleeps on my bladder, pranced up to my chest and looked down on me as if I was her prey, reminding me that it was time for some Purina and water.

I am blessed, I tell you! This man loves me—even though I sleep with a pillow on my chest that makes me look like Jackie Gleason in the sheets—even though I appear to have endured some sort of electroshock therapy in the night and the dog's morning breath is slightly more pleasant than mine.

He is tall and handsome and of Latin descent, but

that's pretty much where the resemblance between reality and my romantic vision ends. We've both been disastrously married before (in both cases for unmentionably brief periods) and grow a little green around the gills when the topic of weddings comes up. Both of us travelled extensively before we got together. We've been to so many of the same places it doesn't really matter that we weren't there with each other. Sitting at home and reading is just fine with us. We both get headaches if we sip cognac. And since my sinuses are no match for Boston winters, my collection of hats is less than glamourous.

Courtship? We haven't had one yet. We were friends. I sat in the church where he married someone else, happy for him and daydreaming that maybe I'd find someone as wonderful as him . . . someday. When his marriage crapped out four months later, I invited him to take walks with me, hoping that he'd talk about the pain that was making him skinnier by the week. We became better friends. I'd stopped by his place of work after a blind date to tell him how awful it was. We'd walk into Cambridge and talk. I had embarked on an ambitious writing project that had nothing to do with paying my rent, and I was forced to leave my beloved home of 10 years in Brookline in search of affordable shelter. We both needed the commiseration then. Hammered by the recession and riddled with insecurity about my career as a writer, I took great comfort in his company, too.

I grabbed work wherever I could find it, typing other people's manuscripts, watching other people's

children, laboring as a caterer and construction work-
er. I was painting an apartment in Watertown for a
contractor buddy of mine—eight bucks an hour and
plenty of time to daydream about things I might have
someday, like health insurance, a full tank of gasoline
and a ready market for these things I feel compelled to
write. It was bleak. I invited the man who would
become my prince to join me in the painting, in hopes
that earning eight bucks an hour *while we commiser-
ated* would seem less dreary. He accepted, we com-
miserated and decided to share the apartment as soon
as the paint was dry.

We arranged the apartment as roommates, but it
was clear we were already partners, veterans of busted
dreams and tough times. We've been living together
more than two years. Our lives are about mutual
support, artistic courage and . . . you know, stuff like
getting the recycling out. It doesn't feel like either of
us has fallen in love. We just love each other. No soft
focus lens, no violin strains or boxes of chocolates. No
wrenching nights, face down on my pillow, no deli-
cious agony when we're apart. No fragile sense of
wellbeing. No champagne wishes or caviar dreams.
Hallelujah!

I wish I could take full credit for this swift move,
but the truth is, if it hadn't crept up on me when I
wasn't expecting anything, I'd never even have noticed it. I might still be divining out perfectly unavailable men: The developmentally stunted . . . the ones
just passing through town . . . the 20-year-olds . . .
and (be still, my heart) the fabulously talented mar-

ried liars. The ones who look like a pump but feel like a sneaker. Ah, l'amour!

Romantic love is about wrenching pain. Like Edith Wharton's *Age of Innocence,* a story that glorifies the creation of the perfect absentee lover whose perfection relies on a continuing absence. Without the annoyances of everyday life, without cohabitation with someone else whose weird quirks challenge the validity of yours, without forgiveness in the face of temporary weight gain due to water retention, this brand of love is available to any neophyte old enough to play Let's Pretend. Believe me, I know.

It's not that true love is a more *passive* form of engagement, though. It's about ambitious undertakings such as learning patience, separating childish dreams about forevermore from here and now, and accepting that there are no guarantees. It's about choosing carefully in the first place and then choosing it again every single day. This ain't for sissies. And songwriters, beware: It doesn't make for great lyrics, either. In fact I think there's only one song title that addresses true love: *I got you, babe.* The real deal doesn't come with a built-in analgesic, like that woozy romantic stuff. It's not like (I always imagined it would be) a non-stop feeling that I may break into a waltz. The truth is that it's more like experiencing small episodes of love for your mate: The minute and a half you watch him reading; the instant you notice he's cleaned off the windshield of your car; when you're with friends and you see they also love him. The rest of the time you can expect to spend in grocery stores, trying to figure out what the hell your beloved is talking about and begging for a massage.

As for longevity, the perfect true love lasts as long as it lasts.

You can look at it this way, or you can follow my 12-step program for slow learners:

1. Suffer needlessly through dozens of ill-fated romances.
2. Excel at self-deception and drama.
3. Crash, burn, spend time in absolute hell.
4. Give up entirely.
5. Get familiar with The Bottom you've hit.
6. Admit you know nothing about anything whatsoever.
7. Get busy with your own goals.
8. Accept a good mate when he/she appears. (Ignore ingrown hairs, dental flaws, etc. Focus on basic goodness.)
9. Vow to include said partner in your sphere, providing things he/she needs and wants, just as you do for yourself.
10. Don't give up when it gets difficult.
11. End up in a house on a hill with a mere mortal for a partner.
12. Get yourself an unbearably cute terrier puppy.

One day at a time, my friends.

French toast and goodbye
A Mother's Day story.

1991

The woman sitting across from me looks a little tired. She's edgy today. Irritated by a headache and eyes that tear easily in the bright May sun. "I forgot my damned sunglasses," she grumbles when the maitre d' seats us at a window table. Then she looks at me warmly as if to apologize. No words are necessary between us—we go back 23 years. And after all this time, the tiniest gesture, quietest sound or just a look says everything.

It's Mother's Day. The woman sitting across from me is taking me out to a fancy brunch. I'm looking at the menu with my eyes scanning left to right, top to bottom, but I'm not reading. All my concentration is being used on retrieving the smallest details of the breakfasts we've had together up until today. On the first day of each of her school years, I took her out. She was always nervous, shy, unable to sleep the night before. She threw up before many of those breakfasts. And most years, she'd sit there as her eggs got cold, telling me how it felt and speaking aloud her worst fears. And the same warm look I saw just now shot back at me over her shoulder then as she took a deep breath and headed into the school yard alone.

This morning, it's me who feels nervous. Because the woman sitting across from me leaves this country in just two weeks to join her fiancé in Africa.

This is, generally, what I raised her to do. To have a big life, to take chances and follow her precious heart. Since her decision to leave, I've felt the most exotic combinations of thrill and loss, of peace and emptiness, independence and abject aimlessness. And the streets of our neighborhood are different to me now. Slightly more hostile, less welcoming in anticipation of her departure.

Last night, I beat her at 500 Rummy as we sipped wine on my balcony and a perfect 75°F breeze rearranged the pink petals that had fallen from the trees. Between the snapping sounds of our playing cards were the two- and three-word references that sent up our laughter, and always will, I reckon.

Today's brunch is marked by odd gestures. We're both letting our bangs grow out, fussing and giving up.

The woman across from me is bothered by the pollen. I can't concentrate on the menu and order French toast as a safe bet when the harried waiter comes. And the sweetest knowing of all this is acknowledged in the snapshot glances, as life goes on, into the mysterious, uncharted future, right on track.